From Göbekli Tepe

Toru Nakamura

Foreword

From Göbekli Tepe is the English edition of my Japanese eBook titled *Gyobekuritepe kara* published in 2013. I present this book in English because the ancient ruins of Göbekli Tepe is drawing world-wide interests lately.

The text of this book is virtually identical to the original book, including the Afterword. However, I have abbreviated the Preface and Chapters 5 and 6 of the original book. Also, I have inserted anew some photos and images which I either photographed for myself or licensed. There was no photo or image in the original Japanese book, except for the one on the cover. Since 2013, there have been a number of news and reports about some new discoveries and losses of archaeological sites in Turkey where the ruins of Göbekli Tepe was discovered. However, most of them had been expected to happen as described in this book.

I wrote a sequel of *Gyobekuritepe kara* which was published in Japanese in 2017 as a paperback book. it is titled *Hebi, Tori to Yume*. Its main focus is on the Chapters 5 and 6 of *Gyobekuritepe kara* and I wrote it from a different angle. Also, the sequel has an appendix of references for authors, books and articles unlike *Gyobekuritepe kara and* this present book. In 2019, I published its English edition which is titled *Snakes, Birds and Dreams: Göbekli Tepe and Caduceus*.

Preface

Today, the world is inundated with news about natural disasters. We see ice sheets and icebergs are melting rapidly in the North and South poles, Greenland, as well as in the high mountains of the Himalayas and the Andes. With fresh water cascading into the ocean, the sea level is rising and the ocean currents are moving off-course and changing their direction of flowing.

The climate of the planet earth has undoubtedly become more volatile and extreme. Torrential rains, cyclones, floods or land slides are frequently taking place in many areas. In other areas, drought, massive forest fires and sand storms are spreading at the same time. Also, catastrophic earthquakes, tsunamis and volcanic eruptions occurred recently within a short period in and around Sumatra, Chile and Japan. These destructive natural phenomena are not coincidently happening by chance.

About 12,000~13,000 years ago, the climate of the planet earth was also changing from the Ice Age to Holocene. As the cold grip began to ease, plants, animals and sea creatures began to thrive in most areas of the temperate zone. So did Homo sapiens (hereafter "Man"), aka modern human. Man's population around this time is estimated to have been about a million.

With the arrival of Holocene on the planet earth, many groups of Man left caves and rocky areas to live in the warmer open field. As foods became abundantly available, Man became more confident for survival and the population grew. Having more time for activities other than hunting and gathering, some of Man spent more time for imagining about the mystery of fertile life, including their own existence.

Looking up to the night sky littered with countless glistening stars and the moon, they began to express their imagination symbolically. The meaning of this symbolic expression could be understood only by Man, who could share it with others at different places and times. It was different from merely drawing the figures of animals or other objects on the rocks as Man used to do in earlier times.

Man's cognitive revolution to communicate with others through symbols gave birth to civilization. Based on many recent archaeological findings, a clear symbolic expression first appeared in and around Göbekli Tepe in southeast Turkey where Eurasia meets Africa. There, archaeologists unearthed stone-carved artefacts with symbolic images and circular structures constructed by massive stone walls and they determined that the construction of Göbekli Tepe's structures began from about 11,500 years ago. It was a pilgrimage site of sorts, more than just an amphitheater, to congregate to share the meaning of Man's newly awakened consciousness about themselves and the hidden presence of supernatural being in nature. Many workers and visitors came to this site

over hundreds of years, giving rise to larger organized communities to plan and cultivate the surrounding area
for foods.

Agriculture undoubtedly opened the door to civilization. However, agriculture could not spread without Man's cognitive revolution and the onset of the mild climate of Holocene. None of these developments happened during the Ice Age. As agriculture spread over wider areas, some of the tribal communities eventually became well-organized societies. This social organization process, however, was often accompanied with violent clashes. In the last century, Man experienced two devastating world wars.

There is a saying that geography determines psychology. The opposite may be true, too. In fact, geography is defined as "the physical features of the earth and its atmosphere, and of human activity as it affects and is affected by them." Today, Man's obsession with growth is changing not only the local climate but also the global climate. Our growth-obsessed world with well over 7 billion people is facing an unprecedented and inseparable twin crisis of the destructive global climate and the violent territorial conflicts over energy, food and other natural resources.

Perhaps, exploring the likely birthplace of our civilization may lead us where our troubled world of today is heading. With this exploratory purpose in mind, I began my journey to Göbekli Tepe with my silent daughter.

Table of Contents

Chapter 1- Northern Mesopotamia 1
The Tigris shore 2
Hasankeyf and Dam 8
East of the Euphrates.. 12
Crossroads of Africa and Eurasia... 20

Chapter 2 World 11~12 Millennia Ago 24
End of the Ice Age.. 25
North and South America: sedentary living............................... 29
Japan: making earthen wares and a figurine 30
Middle East: organizing larger communities 33

Chapter 3- Göbekli Tepe 35
Surrounding geography 36
Unearthed structures and artefacts 42
Mysterious burial and surrounding ruins 52

Chapter 4- Symbolic Cognition and Nature's Fetters 55
Snake, wings and gods 57
Good, evil and one god 62
Man, anthropomorphic gods and Creator................................... 67
Nature exists for Man and the end of the world......................... 72

Chapter 5- Growth and Cyclical Transformation................... 77
Sun, fire and energy 78
Power: from muscles to technology 79

Unmoved Mover and two futures......... 83
Growth and money 85
Energy, urbanization and nature......... 88
Mass production of animals and plants 92
From nuclear to deep sea and the Arctic 94
Chapter 6- Whereabouts of Civilization 99
Living in symbolic consciousness......... 100
Shangri-La and Hakenkreutz......... 102
Bonding on the wane......... 105
Geography determines psychology again......... 107
Stardust in the universe 108
Afterword 114

Chapter 1 Northern Mesopotamia

Diyarbakir in the morning of March 14. After two hours in the air from Istanbul, I arrived at a small local airport in southeast Turkey. Someone should be waiting for me outside the gate. But no one was there to meet with me. Fellow passengers were picked up one by their greeters and all of them were gone after a few hours. While anxiously waiting for someone to show up, I spotted a few people walking towards me. I talked to them in English but they shook their heads. They did not speak English. I had to wait more.

I trusted my English agent to arrange this trip. I did not know the name or place to stay in Diyarbakir. The cold wet March weather made me shiver. I suddenly began to have trepidation. Two weeks earlier, there was a bombing terror in Istanbul by a Kurdish extremist group. After the Assad Syrian government air-raided the area in Homs, the number of Syrian refugees coming to Turkey was increasing. I tried to control my welling doubt. I knew that we would lose our mental balance if we ruminated about the unknown too much.

Fortunately, I found a person who could speak English at a small car rental office at the airport. His name was Mehmed. It is the same name as an Ottoman sultan who conquered Constantinople (today's Istanbul) to end the Byzantine Empire in the 15th century. He helped me, after a few trials. to call the phone number of my English agent in London. Being informed by him about some mishap of communication, I could get a cab to go to my hotel in the city center of Diyarbakir.

A view of the streets seen from the cab was not like Istanbul's at all. Poverty was clearly visible because the city's unpaved streets were muddy and full of large potholes. Suddenly, a little child was running across the street right in front of our cab, forcing me to throw the head backward. Diyarbakir is not far from the border of Iran and Iraq, and most residents in this area are Kurds. Because the Kurdish radical independence movement continued through the 1980's, the central government invested little in this area for a long time, including the streets of this area. But, after some time, wider streets came in sight. Also, there were a few tall buildings with more than 10 stories as well as a few more buildings under construction. My hotel was also a modern building.

The Tigris shore

Exhausted, I wanted to rest a little in the air-heated room before the scheduled evening meeting with my group. But the noise from outside was too loud to sleep. A construction work under way just next to the hotel building. When I opened the window, cold air stroked my tired face and brought back my senses. I decided to go outside to buy a few oranges or bottled water to prepare for the long road trip of the next day.

After a few steps outside the hotel lobby, I saw a US-branded hamburger restaurant and a supermarket,

In the evening, I had a dinner at a restaurant nearby with my fellow travelers, Bülent and Tijen who were our expert guide and travel coordinator, William, Gina, Eiffel and our driver. The dinner started with a lamb entrée and ended with a baklava dessert. Our conversation went smoothly. I could get along with them well, I thought.

In the following morning, a loud noise woke me up. It was a prayer broadcast from the nearby mosque. I opened the window and looked outside. It was cold and damp. It must have rained overnight. I had a quick breakfast of coffee and bread and got out to the van outside to join with the travelling group.

After a while in the van, the view outside began to change. Stone walls over two stories high came in sight. The stone walls were dark blue, almost black. Their distinct color is from the copper-contained basalt. It was not caused by the soot or ageing. These walls were constructed many times over from the fourth century to defend the city from invaders.
They now extend more than five kilometers long.

At present, over 800 thousand residents live in Diyarbakir and its surrounding area. The city of Diyarbakir has a historical record dating back to more than five thousand years. The area was repeatedly occupied by many tribes and kingdoms such as Mitanni, Hittite, Akkad, Assyria, Allam (Bit/Zamani), Media, ancient Persia, ancient Greece (Macedonia), Kurd/Corduene, ancient Rome, Arab, Seljuk, Osman (Ottoman) and others.

During the the Assyrian time, the area was called Amid as inscribed on the scabbard of sword. Later, the Romans called the area as Amida. It was an essential Silk Road trading post because it was at the crossroads where the two civilizations of the East and the West met.

This region has been known as a unique area for its abundance of copper and stone-cutting black obsidian. It is likely that the bronze production by Man may have spread from this region. The known oldest ceramic (fired clay) product unearthed from Mesopotamia was from Tell Halaf located south of Diyarbakir near the present Turkish border with Syria. Using this ceramic producing technique, it was also possible to make bronze, which is a copper-tin metallurgy product. More than five thousand two hundred years ago, the Sumer Kingdom acquired the area's copper and, by adding tin, produced farming tools and weapons made of bronze. Consequently, Sumer became the first ancient society to develop the irrigated agriculture and had the most powerful military force at the time.

We climbed the stairs of the wall structure and looked around the surrounding area. I could see the Tigris River in the distance. Also in sight were the dark-brown colored soil and the yellow green farm lands and fields as far as the eye could see. This location is in the northernmost Mesopotamia and lies between the two large rivers, the Tigris and the Euphrates...the word Mesopotamia means "between two rivers" in Greek.

Looking back to the opposite side, I could see a row of minarets (spired towers) of the Islamic mosque near the center of the city. We were told that one of those towers used to be a tower of the Syriac Church known as the oldest Christian church.

About three thousand years ago and during the Aram Kingdom period, this area was controlled by the Armenian and the Assyrian. These two peoples were rivals but it is known that both converted to Christianity in the 4th century. They did so before the Roman Empire became divided between the Western Roman Empire and the Eastern Roman Empire (Byzantine Empire). The Syriac Church still has a small number of believers today. This church is different from the Catholic Church, the Greek Orthodox Church or the Russian Orthodox Church. Since the 5th century, the latter two churches began to be called the Eastern Orthodox Church.

Amid the intensified confrontation with the Russian after the first World War, millions of Armenians and Assyrians were victimized by the Ottoman Empire's "Union and Progress" policy aimed at minority peoples in this area. Many invasions and wars took place repeatedly in and around Diyarbakir in the ancient times. Even in the 20th century, the same tragedy continued reappear. Mount Ararat, the highest peak in Turkey, soars in the far east of northern Mesopotamia. Today, its foothill near the border with Armenia is assumed by many as the place where the Noah's Ark escaped from the catastrophic flood as the Old Testament describes.

A while later, we headed towards Diyarbakir's central market which used to be a bustling trading post of the Silk Road. Today, its neighborhood was also a busy place. Out of the van and beginning to stroll on the crowded street for a few minutes, a young man approached and asked me "Japon?" In the past few days, I saw many people with a variety of hair and skin colors and faces. But I did not remember seeing any East Asian people. Right behind the main street, there was a large mosque which partially preserved the Romanesque wall built during the Roman Empire time. The mosque is called Ulu Cami. It is the oldest mosque in northern Mesopotamia. There, I saw the inscribed historical records of Diyarbakir about many changing rulers, religions and cultures.

We left the market and headed southeast of Diyarbakir to Hasankeyf, not far from the border with Iraq and Syria. I could see from both sides of our van a vast green farmland spreading over the wet brown-colored soil towards the horizon. We were told that some areas were fields for water melons.

Sitting next to me in the van was William from England. During our long conversation, I learned that he had traveled many known ancient ruins of the world over 40 years.

After more than two hours, the wet green scenery along the Tigris River on the left gradually began to disappear. Instead, small brown-colored mountains and hills began to appear. I then saw a few black oil rigs along the road. Bülent told me that the area was one of the few oil drilling sites in Turkey and that Texaco, a US oil company, owned these rigs.

At present, Turkey's oil supply depends on two sources. One is the tanker-supplied from Russia over the Black Sea to the Bosporus channel. The other is the pipeline-supplied from Azerbaijan and Georgia around the Caspian Sea through the Turkish inland to Seyhan. In recent years, the domestic oil exploration is spreading towards southeast Turkey area close to Iraq.

The van crossed over the canyon and moved on. More than 2,300 years ago, this area was where many ancient united Greek (Macedonian) forces led by Alexander the Great were advancing towards Persia. Suddenly, a cliff dotted with many holes came into view on the left. These holes were caves. In front of their entrances, many stones were piled up. I was told that the dating of these caves was unknown and that they were not natural. The Kurds dug horizontal holes on the cliff and lived in them until recently.

There still exist many unearthed archaeological sites around this area. However, because the Turkish Government tightly regulates archaeological excavation projects, only a few ruins are being unearthed. Also, because the geology of this area is acidic, carbon fossils are difficult to find---woods also tend to decay fast. Nonetheless, archaeologists found stone tools and fossilized animal remains in the caves in the Mediterranean coastal area of Turkey near the border with Syria. Some of them are from the last Ice Age period of around 41 thousand years ago.

Hasankeyf and Dam

Arriving near the peak of the high hill, a city came into sight down below. I could see a minaret of mosque behind the opposite bank of the Tigris River. It stood tall against the gently-sloping mountain. Also, I saw many structures and a steel-framed bridge. The city was Hasankeyf. On the right side of the large bridge was a light brown-colored ruined rock bridge of several tens of meter high against the cliff with many holes. The bridge girder was gone but the piers stood strong in the Tigris River. Its sturdy figure was solid and projected dignity.

We stepped out of the van. In a short distance, I saw a ruined structure. I was told that it used to be a small palace which was reconstructed after having been destroyed by the Mongolian invasion. I also learned that many structures of Hasankeyf had been destroyed by the Mongolian invasion in the mid-13th century. The word Hasankeyf means "rock fortress" in Arabic. During the 7th century when the Arabic occupation of the city began, the name was changed to Hasankeyf. Its name is derived from the fortress which was constructed by the Byzantine Empire in the 4th century.

The Empire tried to protect the city from the Persian invasion. Hasankeyf prospered under the Ayyubids dynasty during the 12th through the early 13th century. The city was crowded with many caravans as a key post for the Silk Road. Since the 16th century, it was ruled by the Ottoman Empire and the present status began since the independence of the Republic of Turkey in 1924.

Looking far beyond the city, I could see a cluster of structures over the hill. Bülent told me that it was developed by the Turkish Government as part of the plan to construct a massive dam called the Ilisu Dam in this canyon. By blocking the massive water flow of the Tigris River, a vast area of the surrounding foothill would submerge under water, so that it was necessary to move a few thousand current residents of Hasankeyf to a new location as seen over the hill. As the dam construction project was opposed both domestically and internationally, the dam project was suspended at present. However, as the demand for electric power and irrigation continued to increase, the crisis facing Hasankeyf to lose its many precious historical ruins was continuing.

Since the 1970s, Turkey constructed many hydropower and irrigation systems in the southeastern Anatolia following the National Government Planning (GAP). So far, the construction of large dams and irrigation projects was completed in and around the Euphrates River, Turkey's another massive river in Mesopotamia. The Atatürk Dam constructed in 1992 was one of the largest dams in the world. Nevalı Çori, one of the ruins nearby, submerged under water by the construction of this dam. The ruins was estimated to be as old as 10,000 years. Furthermore, many other ancient ruins from the time of the Assyrian Empire were also lost by the time when the Birecik Dam construction was completed in June 2000. The surrounding submerged area included Zeugma and a ruins of Samosata. Samosata was once a city of the Roman Empire. In the city of Zeugma, there was a trove of historical treasures, many footprints of the trade and personnel exchanges between the East and the West civilizations.

The world has lost many ruins, not just those in Turkey, by dam construction projects. However, the planned Aswan High Dam project in Egypt began to change the ruinous trend. As it became clear that this project would put the Nubia ruins under water, the United Nations led the world to establish the World Heritage Convention in 1972. The treaty's purpose was to protect and preserve cultural and natural sites of the world. Since then, international assistance began for the archaeological research of ruins. But the final decision would be made by the country concerned. China's Three Gorges Dam construction, the largest dam in the world, was completed in 2009. It is known that its massive construction put many ancient ruins under water, including the residential settlement(s) during the Stone Age and the ruins during the Qin Han through the Ming Qing periods.

As we walked back to the van, many children gathered around us. They were wearing school uniforms. They may have come here for a school tour. I noticed that each of them looked different with black, brown and blond hairs. I suddenly remembered a young waiter I met in the restaurant in Istanbul a few days earlier. When I told him that I was going to Diyarbakir, he said with a very friendly gesture that he was a Kurd and born and raised in Diyarbakir. But because there was no job there, he had to move to Istanbul. He then showed me a photo of his house in Diyarbakir. It stood alone quietly in the field. He said his brothers still lived there.

11

We left Hasankeyf and headed towards Mardin, our next destination. Looking at the moving view outside, I could not help feeling the weight of the history of this area and ruminated about the future of our modern world obsessed with the oil exploration and the dam construction to satisfy our increasing energy needs.

East of the Euphrates

Our van kept climbing the steep hill as the day set in. Soon afterwards, the van stopped on the winding section of the hill and we stepped out. It was sleeting and cold outside. Suddenly, a young man appeared and picked up our bags and ran down the muddy narrow steep road. I was amazed with his strength and speed. It was a surreal superhuman act. We followed him also running in the darkness, trying to avoid the puddle.
Obviously, no car could run on this steep narrow road.

He finally stopped running in front of a solidly-built structure. It turned out to be our hotel...Later I was told that it used to be a mansion owned by a wealthy family. I also learned that other than ourselves, only one couple were staying at this hotel. After I registered my personal information at the counter, I was led to my room from the lobby. To go to my room, I had to climb down the stone steps outside. As I finally came to my room and opened the door, I saw an electric heater was radiating red hot. It was warming the room but it looked dangerous. After somehow managing to settle there, I unplagued and went to bed.

In the following morning around 4 o'clock, the Morning Prayer broadcast from the mosque woke me up. I felt a chill, so I plugged back the heater and stayed in bed for a while. As the day light seeped into the room, I got up and stepped out to the balcony. The floor was coated with a thin layer of fresh snow. Far out beyond a row of structures seen below the balcony, a fertile land covered with early spring greens spread as far as the eyes could see. Mardin was a small city built on one of the few hills in the vast plain of northern Mesopotamia. I learned that the name Mardin meant "fortress" in Aramaic (Armenia), which again reminded me of this area's long tumultuous history with many recurrent wars. Later, as I was walking outside, I found that the muddy puddles became frozen overnight. As I carefully walked on it, I saw some road paving work was in progress. Nearby, I could buy a few oranges at a small corner grocery shop as it was just opening the day's business.

After breakfast, we got in the van to go down the snow-covered road. We were heading to the Deyulzafaran Monastery. On the way, we stopped and took a walk to see the ruins of the irrigation facilities and tombs which Roman Empire had built and left. I learned that the area was where the the soldiers of the Roman Empire stationed in the 4th century. In Turkey, there are many ruins of structures in Turkey which the Roman Empire built. The Empire built a key transportation network extending from the Mediterranean coast to the eastern Turkey because it was imperative to move and put a great many goods and people in order to control the widening area.

"The same thing happened in Europe," said William...In fact, a recent research showed that the Roman Empire had built many forts with rock walls in today's Scotland, Germany, Rumania and the northern Africa (Algeria) during the late 5th century BCE through the 2nd century. Many of these forts were more than four meters high and three meters thick. Most of them, except a small number of them, are gone today. However, the total wall barrier built by the Roman Empire was longer than the China's Great Wall which was also built around the similar period.

At a distance about a few miles south of Mardin, I could see a large structure with light reddish-brown color appeared over the hill against the sleet-mixed rainy sky. It was the Deyulzafaran Monastery. Its dreamlike structure standing in isolation was once a monastery-church of the Assyrians, where they worshipped the sun god 3-4 thousand years ago. They later rebuilt it after their conversion to the Syriac Christianity. The structure was repeatedly renovated after the 5th century. I was also told that the name Deyulzafaran was derived from the reddish-brown color of saffron, which was the crop grown in the surrounding area.

Inside the monastery and down the stone steps, there was a low-ceiling room. Its wall faced east and had a small window from where the light peeped through from outside. I was told that it was the place where the Assyrians worshipped the sun god. The low ceiling was made of a few huge long solid stones. Our guide explained that the Assyrians had built the floor of Syriac praying area on top of those ceiling stones.

On the way back in the afternoon, the entire city of Mardin came into sight through the window of the moving van. As I was watching the city built over a small mountain against the grey sky, the sleet began to change to snow. On a clear blue-sky day, the city must become a shining city on the hill. We stopped at a mosque before going back to our small hotel. Outside the mosque, there was a square-shaped pond on the stonebuilt structure. Water flowing from the east entered into the pond through a narrow channel. The pond symbolizes the life completed going to heaven.

Before the sunset, we visited a house at the hidden corner on the hilly slope of Mardin. It was a home where a woman of Syriac Christian faith lived. We were told that she had been awarded by the Turkish Government for her 90th birthday and she spent everyday painting by imagination many stories in the Bible. We entered into the room where she spent most her time. She showed us her painted figure of Christ on the cross on a large fabric spreading over the room. It was her proud work of art.

At present, the population of Mardin is about 80 thousands. Most of them are Muslims. The number of Syriac Christians is about 300. However, many other Syriac Christians visit the Deyulzafaran Monastery from all over the world. Also, young people from Sweden come every summer to learn at the Monastery. So I was told.

South of Mardin, near the border with Syria, there is a ruins of Tell Halaf where the oldest fired earthenware in Mesopotamia was discovered in the early 20th century. Since 2006, a new excavation project began in and around Tell Halaf. It is expected that there are many other unearthed ruins older than five thousand years in the surrounding area. Already, a number of stone-carved figurines of women and cows of around eight thousand years old were unearthed. Also discovered there were clay tablets etched with cuneiform characters (Hurrian letters). These letters were used by the Hurrian people who lived there about 5 thousand years ago. In the future, many riddles of the ancient society will likely be solved by these excavations of ruins around Mardin.

In the following day, we headed west from Mardin on a straight highway. It was very windy. The wind often jolted and pushed the van sideways. Trucks coming from the opposite lane were also moving like snakes. This area is windy in spring. Were the caravans in ancient times also traveling in this severe environment? After a while, a vast cottongrowing field spreading along the highway came in sight.

The plains of Harran which means "road" in Akkadian expands from the west of Mardin to the east of the Euphrates River. The present road network in Harran was constructed over the roads originally built by the Roman Empire. Harran was a city where the civilizations of the East and the West interacted and prospered since Seleucus, a general under Alexander the Great, began to control the area. It is also known that the people of Harran embraced Christianity before others did.

An Islamic university campus existed in Harran in the late 8th century. I was told that it was the oldest and leading academic institution to teach astronomy, philosophy and medicine around that time. Harran University, a new university, was built in the same location in the late 20th century. At its vast campus, I found a stone monument with the moon and the star carved on it like the national flag of the present Turkey. There were many young people there, including some on camel-back. It might be a spring break for students. Our friendly guide who was a student of the University took us to a small hill nearby. There was a large ruins whose structure was partially collapsed. I learned that the Hittite worshipped the sun god there four thousand years ago. Its stone ceiling was partially reconstructed. As I looked up at the ceiling, I saw a cross embedded in the center of the ceiling. It showed a clear record of the arrival of Christianity which came there more two thousand years later.

The city of Urfa (şanrlurfa in Turkish) is just north of Harran. Urfa was ruled by many different peoples from ancient times like Diyarbakir and Mardin. However, today, Urfa is a city with modern roads and hotels. Its location is about 200 kilometers from the eastern shore of the Mediterranean Sea. About a half million people live in the city in a warm area unlike the inland area of northern Mesopotamia.

Urfa has been known as Edessa during the Byzantine Empire period, today, a large-scale aqueduct supplying abundant water from the Euphrates River is being constructed for the agriculture of the surrounding area and the citizens of Urfa. Urfa was once an oasis blessed with spring water. It is sometimes called the City of Prophets because this place is likely the birthplace of major religions. In fact, Urfa is said to be the birthplace of

Abraham, who was the father of the Jews and teacher of Judaism, Christianity and Islam as well.

When we came to one of the corners of the city's center, Gina, an Israeli, looked particularly excited to come to this place. It was a wooded park with a pond. The pond is called "Sacred Pond." As I approached to the pond, I saw many people around this sacred area. A few people sat at the edge of the pond. While many were talking, others seemed to be meditating. The place is believed to be where God saved Abraham from burning at the stake. Because the fired fagots suddenly fell into this pond and turned to fish. I saw many grey-colored fish swimming in the clearwater pond.

Adjacent to the pond was a bustling market packed with families. There were many shops selling döner kebab (lamb meat cooked on a vertical rotisserie) and plenty of red or yellow spices. After a while through a labyrinthine market, I walked into a courtyard crowded with people enjoying coffee or tea. The place might have been for the caravan traveling on the Silk Road in ancient times. I saw men with Keffiyeh head scarfs enjoying board and card games. While William and I were watching their games, a few smiling people approached and began to talk us. This peaceful area was one of the bases for the Crusaders in the 12th century and also for the Turkish independence movement from the English and French occupation after the First World War

The ruin of Göbekli Tepe was discovered in 1994 by a sheep herder on the hill from about 15 kilometers from the city of Urfa. Later, it became clear that the ruin had been built from around 11,500 years ago. It was discovered on a gentle hill surrounded by the vast irrigation system which was developed east of Birecik Dam built over the Euphrates River.

Considering the fact that many ancient ruins submerged under water from the construction of Birecik Dam, its discovery was extremely fortunate because the subsequent study in and around Göbekli Tepe is beginning to upend the conventional view about the history of civilization or humanity. It will also enable us to know better where our world of today is heading in the future.

Crossroads of Africa and Eurasia

The Turkey-Syria border stretches from the Mediterranean Sea across the Euphrates River. It is also where the three earth plates of Africa, Eurasia and Arabia intersect. The area south of the border surrounded by the Mediterranean Sea and the desert of the Arabian Peninsula is known as the Levantine corridor (Levant). It is where the plants and the animals of each continent migrate in and out, forming a rare and extremely rich natural environment of both the flora and the fauna.

In 1993, archaeologists from Japan and Syria unearthed the fossilized remains of a young Neanderthal (hominin) in the Dederiyeh Cave located about 60 kilometers east of Aleppo in northwest Syria. This remains as well as other discovered Neanderthal remains were found in Levant.
They are 65 to 47 thousand years old. However, archaeologists have not discovered the fossilized remains of Man (homo sapiens) in Levant in the same period. It was very cold in Levant during the Ice Age. Even if small groups of Man tried to migrate north to Levant from Africa, many of them could not compete with the Neanderthal men who lived there. Neandertals

could withstand the severe cold climate during the Ice Age with their physically strong bodies covered with abundant hairs.

Man or Homo sapiens is a distinct surviving hominin and different from Homo-erectus. All of us living today on earth are Man, whose ancestors emerged in Africa about 200 thousand years ago. Although there are some disagreements about this estimated time, it is more or less accepted now. Since then, some groups of Man journeyed out of Africa...in 2007, a fossilized hominin jaw bone as old as 100 thousand years ago was discovered but it is likely to be Neanderthal's or other non-surviving hominin's.

About 70 thousand years ago, a truly catastrophic natural disaster took place in and around the area known as the Toba Lake in Indonesia. Considered to be the largest eruption ever recorded in the history of the earth, it destroyed an enormous area of the living environment for plants and animals. Studies on geological strata confirmed that the massive amount of volcanic ashes had reached the stratosphere and that the falling ashes accumulated over much of the land in Southeast Asia, India and Africa. Its destructive effect continued for a long time. With no sunlight in the following few years, the atmospheric temperature severely dropped.

According to some scholars, some of Man in Africa survived the catastrophe. However, the population of Man is estimated to have declined to less than 10 thousands at one point. Also, by around 50 thousand years ago, some of their descendants are thought to have migrated out of Africa. This time estimate is not based on the dating method applied to the fossilized remains. Instead, it is derived from the sequencing analysis of mutations (marker change) in the Y chromosome left in the DNA and from the mathematical application of probability theory. The DNA samples were extracted from a number of native men in isolated communities of today in various regions of the world. Man's population exceeds over 7 billion today and all of us are the descendant of those who left out of Africa. This ingenious finding about the history of Man to populate the planet earth owes largely to the pioneering study of Luigi Luca Cavalli-Sforza.

By the time to move out of Africa, Man possessed sharp piercing and cutting weapons made of bones and stones (spears, bows and arrows, cut stones, etc.). By wielding them and working as a team, Man hunted and continued to live successfully. On the other hand, Neanderthals, unlike Man, did not hunt and work as a team so that they were overwhelmed by Man. As a result, their population gradually dwindled and disappeared before around 20 thousand years ago.

As years passed by, each descendant group of Man migrated from the Arabian Peninsula in all directions to Caucasus, Central Asia, India and East Asia. Most of them in the distance eventually began to totally lose contacts with others because they moved on foot during the Ice Age. Over many generations, their physical characteristics gradually began to change. With occasional genetic mutations peculiar in each descendant group, the color of skin or hair, height and other physical features became distinct, which also reflect the different climate and ecological conditions of each specific area where they lived.

As the Ice Age receded and Holocene arrived, the natural environment of the region called the "Fertile Crescent" was particularly productive for life. With the region's mild climate and rich soil stretching from Mesopotamia to Levant, Man's food resources of plants and animals abundantly propagated there. As the ice sheets and icebergs in the mountainous area of Caucasus began to melt, many groups of Man living in the flooded area must have also migrated south to northern Mesopotamia. During this transition period, the spectacle of Göbekli Tepe began to appear in northern Mesopotamia. The time of this coming was about 11,500 years ago when the last Ice Age was ending.

In recent years, many hitherto unknown archaeological sites have been discovered all over the world. Some are as old as Göbekli Tepe's ruins, if not older. A number of ruins discovered or lost in Mesopotamia teach us about the ancient culture's deep connection with their surrounding physical features of nature...nature shaped the local society which developed in and around it. So, if there is a far-reaching change in nature, locally-developed cultures will eventually change to become a regional or global culture or civilization. My interest in Göbekli Tepe continued to grow. What was taking place in Man's other areas of the world 11,500 years ago when the spectacle of Göbekli Tepe began to appear in northern Mesopotamia?

Chapter 2 World 11~12 Millennia Ago

Rock art and artefacts discovered in many archaeological sites reveal how Man cognized his/her existence or life during the Ice Age. Among them are rock wall murals discovered in Australia and Southern Europe and many of the stone-carved figurines and clay statues unearthed in Middle East and Asia. Some of them are 30~40 thousand years old. It is estimated that the vivid images of Man's hunting scene found in the caves in France and Spain were painted 17~12 thousand years ago.

The well-known cave art of Lascaux Cave in France painted Man's hunting scene, wielding spears to kill animals. However, there was no distinct image to reveal Man's inner psychology in the painted scene, except for the place of Man's life being expressed at the same level as the animal's. However, as the fertile world spread when the Ice Age was ending, Man's cognition of life and death began to change visibly. Man could spend less time to hunt and compete for foods for their families and more time to imagine for non-physical activities. As the surrounding natural environment made it easier to secure foods, some of them must have thought about the lives of others and animals taken for their own survival after gory killings.

During the Ice Age, the media used to express Man's imaginations or observations were stone, wood or clay. The expressed images by Man were not the same because the media used were not only different but also the communication was not possible as they lived in geographically distant areas. However, as the Ice Age was ending and the natural environment changed, similar creative activities began to appear as Man tried to express their cognition of existence or life and death. After many thousands of generation passed after Man left out of Africa, Man's imagination about their existence began to reflect the changing climate and geology of the earth.

End of the Ice Age

After the Ice Age receded, the climate of the planet earth gradually turned warmer. In the temperate zone, the atmospheric temperature became mild and relatively stable, except for the seasonal change of each year. Earth scientists call this new post-Ice Age period of the planet earth as the Holocene epoch. However, the climate during this transition period was unstable at times, particularly during a few thousand years from around 14 thousand years ago. During this period, the Northern Hemisphere was going through an extremely cold period called Younger Dryas. It was triggered by the changing ocean current as the iceberg in and around Arctic melted. However, the Ice Age, more precisely speaking the last Ice Age, ended by around 11,500 years ago.

During the Ice Age, the Eurasian continent was connected with the North American continent via the island of Beringia located in the present Bering Strait. During the Ice Age, about 30 percent of the land of the earth was covered with ice and, in some area, the ice was thicker than 3 kilometers.

The Eurasian continent was also connected then with the Japanese archipelago in the north, so that many herds of large animals migrated over land from Sakhalin to Hokkaido. Today, the ice-covered land area of the earth has already shrunk to about 10 percent. As the global warming progresses, the ice-covered area will no doubt shrink further.

Global sea level around 20 thousand years ago was more than 100 meters lower than today's level. We can only imagine how the borderlines between the land and the sea, rivers and lakes moved when ice sheets and icebergs began to melt. Some coastal land areas either submerged under water or rose like the fjords of Scandinavia. Naturally, the terrains of many areas were quite different from those of today. Change came not only in the geology but also in the ecosystem and the physical appearance of Man among different groups as well because they dispersed far and wide and separated each other for a long time since leaving Africa.

The dramatic change in climate began around 13~14 thousand years ago. It became known from the changing glacial geology of Greenland, Antarctic, etc. According to many studies, the extracted samples from the icebergs clearly showed the increased pollen concentration in this period as the content of sands had decreased, which means that the dehydrated weather had become hydrated. Moreover, the rainfall in Northern Hemisphere was the heaviest around 11,500 years ago, aside from regional differences. Also, during this dramatic climate change, earthquakes, fault movements and volcanic eruptions frequently took place around the borderlines where the major earth plates intersected.

When the Ice Age was ending, volcanoes in the southern Alaska such as Mt. Redoubt likely erupted continuously near the borderline between the Pacific Plate intersected with the North American Plate. Also, the midsteam area of the Yukon River (north of the same area) was a vast grassland covered by ice sheets and icebergs. It took many thousands of years for today's vast forests of many conifers, birch, willow and poplar to begin to spread in this boreal zone.

Volcanic eruptions were also frequently taking place in the Japanese archipelago where the three large earth plates of the Pacific, the North American and the Philippine intersected. Mt. Fuji seen today was shaped by a number of massive volcanic eruptions which lasted for several thousand years since around 13,000 years ago. The volcanic ashes accumulated over time to become the black soil (Andosols) which made it difficult for most plants, other than the Japanese pampas grass and bamboo, to absorb phosphate. For this reason, the flora in Japan changed very slowly even as the climate became warm. Although the Kinki and Shikoku region was different due perhaps to the fact that there were (are) no volcano around the region, It is estimated that it took 4~5 thousand years for a new flora to spread through north of the Kanto region over the Japanese archipelago.

Around the same time, it is inferred that the area where the earth plates of Africa, Arabia and Eurasia intersected continued to be inundated with heavy rainfalls as the temperate zone warmed. The sea levels frequently changed, flooding the coastal areas of both the Mediterranean and the Black Sea. So, much of the lowland of the Mediterranean Sea coast submerged under water. The geological evidence of these floods was found in Levant. According to Ofer Bar-Yosef's study, steppe and forests appeared over the arid area (desert), increasing the amount of water in many lakes or even creating new lakes there. Also, the lake bottom terrain showed that in the same period a huge earthquake had taken place in and around today's Lebanon. Also known is the fact that Mt. Sűphan Dagi in eastern Turkey where a massive earthquake took place in 2011 had frequently erupted in the same period,

By around 11,500 years ago, a mild climate spread over the coastal area of the Mediterranean Sea ahead of other areas. In the Fertile Crescent of grasslands and gentle hills, wild wheat species and other annuals known for their numerous seeds propagated and spread widely. In addition to the mild climate, an especially fertile earth (soil) was created there by the two surrounding huge rivers, the Euphrates and the Tigris, which flow south to the Persian Gulf from Northeast Turkey south of the Caucasus Mountains. Levant is known to have an especially diverse ecosystem created by the seasonally changing mixture of Eurasian and African floras and faunas. Even today, the number of animal species found in northern Syria and Turkey (Anatolia) is estimated about 80 thousands, exceeding the estimated number of about 60 thousands in the entire Europe.

With a remarkable change in the earth's geology and ecosystem, Man living in many areas of the world could afford spending less time and energy to hunt animals and gather plants for survival. A larger group of Man equipped with stone tools cut by obsidian and quartz appeared and began to efficiently exploit and utilize the hunted or collected food and clothing resources. Man's knowledge about these resources, their location and the time of their appearance increased. In this process, many groups of Man were freed from the way of living to always spend time to look for foods.

North and South America: sedentary living

When the Ice Age was ending, the climate of the temperate and subarctic zones in the northern Hemisphere was fluctuating violently. North America was particularly affected by changing ocean currents caused by the melting Arctic ice. Man, the hunter and gatherer, had already migrated to South America from Siberia via Alaska during the Ice Age. The ruins of Monte Verde discovered in Chile is estimated to be about 12,500 years old. Based on the unearthed hearth traces, a small group or groups of Man not only hunted large animals but also small animals, gathered various nuts like chestnut, fished and harvested seashells

In North America, archaeologists found a ruins of a dwelling of 11,500 years old in the Tanana forest in Alaska in summer 2010. In this ruins called Xaasaa Na', a fractured cranial-bone (skull) of a cremated young child of about 3 years old was unearthed. Also discovered some pits which likely had poles in them to support the dwelling structure, a hearth as well as a waste disposal site. According to Ben Potter of University of Alaska, the place was likely used during summer and but it was abandoned after the child died. It is the oldest evidence so far to show Man's presence in North America. In addition, because there were numerous small sharply-cut stones and fossilized bones of small animals such as salmons, squirrels and grouses at the site, it is likely that the place was a sedentary site rather than a temporary camp site temporarily set up in search of large animals such bison or elk.

At the ruins of Xaasaa Na', the child's cranial bone was placed in the dwelling's center surrounded by two loess blocks (ochers), which are created only by volcanic eruptions. It suggests that the dead child was buried and sanctified there. There must be other ruins to prove Man's presence in Alaska in earlier times. However, it is difficult to find them in Alaska because the terrains significantly changed by melting glaciers and volcanic eruptions.

Japan: making earthen wares and a figurine

During the Ice Age, the Japanese archipelago was also connected over land with the Eurasian continent like the North American continent. Many groups of Man in the archipelago were also hunters and gatherers and lived in and around the caves. One of the oldest archaeological sites in the Japanese archipelago is the Iwashuku ruin (in Gunma Prefecture), where 20 thousand-years-old cutting stone tools were unearthed. The Japanese archipelago has many volcanoes like Alaska, so that it has been difficult to find other ruins which existed in the transitional time from the Ice Age to Holocene.

Most ruins discovered in Hokkaido and Tohoku, the northern area of the archipelago, are 5~6 thousand years old as described earlier. However, in recent years, archaeologists found some ruins and earthen wares which are older than 10 thousand years. Also, according to the 2011 genetic study of the rice found there, the Japonica rice had already cultivated during the same period. It has upended a conventional view that the rice cultivation in Japan began around 2,500 years ago via China.

In 2010, archaeologists discovered the ruin of Aidani-Kumahara near the Aichi River in Shiga Prefecture of the Kinki region. Some section of the ruin is estimated to be 13 thousand years old. As described earlier, the Kinki region was not covered by the black soil (Andosols). So, the flora was relatively rich and diverse, which made it easier to find foods and settle. In the unearthed ruin, there were numerous pits for pit-house dwellings, fired earthen wares and eoliths (chopping stones) and one clay figurine of a woman. The figurine was three centimeters tall with an exaggerated breasts. It is the oldest figurine found in Japan. She was made to stand upright. This small figurine was likely an amulet and not an ornament made for any ceremonial purpose.

The fired earthen vessel could keep water from leaking out, making it possible to boil or steam fish, small animals, shells, nuts and vegetables. According to the Australian archaeologist Gordon Child, the fired earthenware was the first invention of Man to exploit the special chemical property of materials.

Other ruins of discovered in recent years in Japan were also as old. In1995, archaeologists discovered the ruins of Hanamiyama. Some earthen wares unearthed are estimated to be 11~12 thousand years old, when the Ice Age was ending. They include fired earthen wares with a few linear symbols, which are the oldest symbols found in Japan. In this ruin, archaeologists also found a pit-house dwelling site just like ruins of Xaasaa Na' in Alaska, spears (pointers) and knives made of andesite as well as their production site. In 2009, archaeologists unearthed the ruin of Torigake Nishikaizuka in Chiba Prefecture. There, they discovered not only earthen wares but also a dozen of fossilized bones of boar and deer. The ruin is about 10 thousand years old. These bones were placed next to earthen wares, they suggest that some spiritual activity was performed there to sanctify the hunted animals.

Man sanctified the power of woman to give birth or the life of animals he took for food. This cognitive reverence was universal for all Man through the end of the Ice Age. However, recent interdisciplinary and global researches and studies of archaeology, geology, genetics researches, etc., are beginning to shed new light to Man's emerging vision of the world when the Ice Age was ending.

Middle East: organizing larger communities

In the late Ice Age period of 14~12 thousand years ago, there were a number of sedentary groups of Man called Natuf who lived along the shores of the Euphrates and the Jordan River in Levan...during the same period when the ruin of Aidani-Kumahara existed. It is estimated that about a small number, likely a few dozen, Natufians began to live not only by hunting but also by sedentary foraging unlike the mobile huntergatherers. In and around these Natufian ruins, there were some fossilized wild wheats with some traces of uniform genetic changes, which suggests that there was some activity to secure foods by manipulating the wild nature. Based on these and other findings led by Ofer Bar-Yosef and Donald Henry, it is inferred that some of the Natufians may have tried to seed and cultivate wheats by the end of the 12th millennium ago.

Near the shore of the Euphrates River in Syria, there was a ruin called Tell Abu Hureyra. It was a Natufian community, which is estimated to have existed intermittently for a few thousand years until around 9,000 years ago, a time of transition from the Ice Age to Holocene. It submerged under water now because a dam was constructed. However, it was not a continuously inhabited site because the climate during this period was severely cold and unstable. Under such harsh condition, large migrating animals like gazelle were difficult to find and hunt, so that it was not possible to maintain the sedentary way of living. However, when the climate became milder and stable, the same area was re-inhabited and the community began to grow larger.

33

By around 9,000 years ago, many sedentary communities, each with a few hundred residents, began to appear in the Fertile Crescent. These communities not only cultivated cereals but also domesticated large animals such as cattle and sheep by repeatedly crossbreeding them. They domesticated these animals for food and, later, the cattle became indispensable for expanding the area of cultivation. In this process, it became also possible for some communities to build large food storage structures made of fired clay. As a warmer and stable summer season spread in the Mediterranean coast, they could store not only cereals and beans but also dried or smoked meats.

Until recently, the temple of Uruk in southern Mesopotamia (present Iraq) was thought as the oldest ruin of either temple or shrine where people congregate to worship. It is estimated to be around 6,500 years old. Also, conventional knowledge about the history of religion, including the description in the Old Testament, left few clues about how it developed and spread. Against this background, the organized region was often thought to have followed agriculture because agriculture requires a common belief or purpose to organize people and maintain social order. However, some ruins and artefacts recently discovered in Near and Middle East upends this conventional knowledge. Among them, the most important discovery is the ruin of Göbekli Tepe near the Euphrates River in southeastern Turkey.

Chapter 3 Göbekli Tepe

The site around the old known ruin at Göbekli Tepe was reexamined by Klaus Schmidt of German Archaeological Institute (Deutches Archäologisches Institut). At the request of the Turkish Government, he and other German and Turkish archaeologists carefully began excavating the ruins since 1994. The excavation will continue for many more years. Schmidt expressed his view or theory about the ruins based on his findings up to 2007. Following is the gist of his talk about the ruin at Göbekli Tepe:

The area looked different from today's then. From the environmental point of view as well as from the unearthed fossilized plants and animal bones, it was a very fertile area where many mammals, green fields, forests and abundant water existed. It was like a paradise. Many people came to build this site. After constructing the facility, they probably prayed here as a group for sanctifying the deceased. As more visitors came to the site, it became necessary to secure more foods. So, it is likely that they began to cultivate over the surrounding hills to produce more foods. In other words, agriculture spread from here to a wider area in order to perform and support the ritual at this site. However, perhaps it also caused their demise.

Schmidt's use of the last word "demise" is intriguing because he did not elaborate his thought. In any way, Schmidt also thought that there might be a tomb at the site because he found a carved large stone slab with a niche (recessed part of a wall), which looked like a door. His view cannot be dismissed because the artefact known as "false door" existed in ancient Egypt...the dead pharaoh's spirit entered into a different world from this door. A similar stone slab was unearthed in 2010 from the tomb site in Luxor in Egypt. It is estimated to be about 3,500 years old. Obviously, the future excavation will tell us whether or not the slab unearthed at Göbekli Tepe was indeed a false door.

Surrounding geography

Göbekli Tepe is located about 15 kilometers east from Urfa and close to the Euphrates River in southeastern Turkey near the border with Syria. The surrounding ground is covered with white limestones formed during the Eocene period. Under the surface of the ground, there is a very hard nodular stratum, which looks yellow in spots with fossilized microorganism. The physical feature in and around Urfa/Harran region was created by the Euphrates River's meandering flows with sediment running down south from the Taurus Mountains in the north. Its ground is generally flat although there are low hills.

In the ancient time, people traveling between Levant and Mesopotamia faced a difficult problem of how to cross the huge Euphrates River. If they wanted to avoid crossing the Euphrates, they had to either travel north through hilly mountainous areas more than 400 hundred kilometers or travel south equally for a long distance through the Arabian Desert to go to the Persian Gulf area. When traveling was possible only on foot or with caravans, it was likely that some people risked to cross the Euphrates by log rafts in order to save travelling time.

About 2400 years ago (4th century BCE), Seleucus known as a "Diadochi" (successor in Greek) of Alexander the Great built a city called Zeugma (bridge in Greek) on the Euphrates River's shore of about 50 kilometers west of Urfa. Today, much of the city submerged under water after the Birecik Dam was built.

Before the Dam was completed, a French archaeological team was researching around the ruins at the request of the Turkish Government. In their research report in 2000, the travel route used by the ancient caravans was seen on the basis of the satellite image of the terrain. The French report also suggested that the religion, philosophy or science of the Eastern world that had impacted the Western world may have come to the area of Zeugma first, eventually reaching the Ionian region and then spread to the wider Western world...Losing this historically important site is regrettable because it is no longer possible to discover the archaeological materials to improve our understanding of how the East-West cultural exchange in and around this region influenced the world of civilization.

If the Euphrates River region is developed further just for economic development, more hitherto undiscovered ruins may be lost. The world may lose more than the ruins of Zeugma. Some may be comparable to the ruin of Göbekli Tepe. In fact, the ruins of NevalI çori located north of Göbekli Tepe and Tell Abu Hureyra have already submerged under water. What may be lost is not just the ruins of importance to be discovered. The geological change caused by constructing more dams, irrigation systems and electric power facilities will not only alter the local culture but also bereave the region of the nature's benefits in the long run. Already, the Euphrates River's water flow has changed, contaminated the water and raised the underground water level. The increased salt content in the recycled irrigation water will certainly create a serious problem. This problem has already occurred in the irrigated inland regions in California.

In front of our van, I saw a road sign board spelled "Göbekli Tepe." The van ran up a gently sloped road through an area with some small trees on the right. We stopped near the top of a hill covered with light-brown limestones and short grass.

As I getting out of the van, I saw a dog looking at us in front of a small structure. It had a solar panel and a satellite dish on the roof. It turned out to be the management office. Nearby, there was also an open entrance to the ruin of Göbekli Tepe. When Bülent, our guide, talked to a person of the office, William and I were anxiously waiting to walk up the hill. Looking around the site while I was waiting, I could see the ridgeline far out on the horizon.

Soon, I began to understand the reason why people had decided to create a spectacle at this site. It was the terrain and geology of this site. There was no doubt in my mind that it must have taken innumerable time and work to construct many structures on this site. According to the research and study conducted so far, the time and work required to construct this site were estimated to be at least several years even with hundreds of workers.

The word Göbekli Tepe means "potbelly hill" in Turkish. Indeed, this place is at the center of a gently spreading hill and there are ruins underneath the ground of the hill. The total area of the ruin discovered so far is estimated to be about 22 acres (8,900 square meters). Also, Schmidt and others concluded that after about a thousand years later, their creation was intentionally buried under ground to create this potbelly hill. It must have taken time and work to bury, not destroy, many structures underground. The ruins remained invisible underground for many thousands of years through late 20th century.

The excavation of the ruin of Göbekli Tepe led by Schmidt began in 1995. So far, only a small portion was unearthed. According to the research conducted by special radar and geomagnetic tools, it is estimated that the total area of the ruin of Göbekli Tepe consists of about 20 circular structures, including a few which have already been unearthed. A young guide of the site told us that the excavation was not done currently but it would begin in April when the weather becomes milder. The Schmidt's group will continue to excavate the area carefully. Their work is not going to end anytime soon. It will certainly take many more years or decades.

Unearthed structures and artefacts

The walkway from the gate towards the potbelly hill was the bedrock of white and light brown colors. On the right of the walkway, there was a flat bedrock. When I looked at it carefully, I saw a large hole of perhaps a few meters in diameter and in depth as well. The rim of the hole was trimmed by about a foot deep.

Right next to the hole, there was a relief-like spot which resembled a pitted half-fruit. Its diameter might be one and a half meters. In addition, there were many smaller holes of 10~30 centimeters in diameter. Among them, there were four large holes, each of which was placed at each corner of a square of a few meters long each side. Large logs must have been placed in them as pillars or poles. They may have supported the roof or the walls of some structure.

There is no doubt that Göbekli Tepe was the place for many people to congregate for some spiritual experience. According to the research and study done so far, there was no settlements nearby, which indicates that people who visited the site were from distant places. However, there was no evidence so far to show that the place was a tomb site.

As I continued to walk on the bedrock road, I saw a large steep slope on the right side. It looked like a spectator area of an amphitheater. Although the surrounding area was a bedrock with lime stones, the slope was covered mostly with sandy soil. The slope was too steep to climb down. Since the potbelly hill is situated on the top of the slope, it is possible that the ruins were buried with the sandy soil taken from this sloped area.

After a few minutes, I saw an excavation area. I was told that a corner on the left was the very spot where Şafak Yildiz, a sheep herder, accidentally found a protruding stone on the ground in 1994. He thought it had looked different from other stones on the ground. As I kept walking, I saw stone walls of several meters high. Within the circle surrounded by these walls, there were several stone pillars. Some were covered by wooden boxes which might be for protecting the spots around some carved animals.

According to Bülent, what Yildiz found was the tip of a large stone which was partially broken at its top. As I stepped further onto the excavation site, I saw a few tall stone statues among a number of stone artefacts. There was a wooden suspension aisle which was firmly tied with wires and pipes inside the excavation site to keep people away from walking on the excavated ground. I suddenly recalled Schmidt's words...there may be a tomb beneath the carved stone statues. At the high spot of the circular site, I saw a pair of large T-shaped stone pillars. They were nearly identical and looked at least five meters tall, standing above some stone-carved animals.

As I approached one of them closely, the image of hands came into my view. I saw five carved fingers in each hand and two long arms on both sides of the pillar. The arms were carved up to the top of the pillar. It was clearly created in the image of a Man. The top of this T-shape statue must be his or her head. Other images carved in the statue were a band and a cloth to hide the private parts around the hip area. Judging from the statue's size and height and also considering that they wore elaborately designed garments, it is likely that this T-shaped statue was a symbol of a special being, either a Man to perform a ritual or an anthropomorphic god or goddess.

According to the articles written by Schmidt and others, the animals carved on stone pillars surrounded by the circular stone walls were snake, boar, fox, panther (lion?), bear, bison, crane, aurochs, gazelle, equus hemionus (Asian donkey), mouflon (wild sheep), condor and scorpion. These animals must have exited in the area around 11,500 years ago. These animals were either sedentary in the area or migrating over the Harran plain north and south at the turn of season. Judging from the amounts of their bones excavated, workers and visitors ate aurochs more than a half of all the meats they consumed at the site.

William and I walked up the hill to the back of the circle of the excavated site. The view behind the hill looked almost the same as what I saw earlier in the opposite direction near the entrance. I looked around with my telescope. Below the horizon, I saw a spot under excavation. It was dug as a square pit which was divided in nine sections. I saw some stone structures in some of them. When I started to walk towards the fence, a strong wind suddenly hit my face. I could hardly stand up. Then, I heard a voice telling me not to enter. Perhaps, the voice was from one of the office personnel.

I was told that only four spots in the ruin had been excavated so far, including the one under excavation. Soon after, I saw a structure covered with galvanized roof over the excavated site...It might be where some of the excavated artefactss were temporarily stored because inside that structure, there were some solid materials which looked like stone-carved artefacts.

As we walked back and returned to the entrance area, Bűlent introduced us one of the personnel of the office. He turned out to be a son of Şafak Yildiz. According to his explanation, his father also found a stone-carved figurine of a man of penile erection. He said it was stored in the museum of Urfa although it was not displayed. Suddenly, a flash crossed my mind: Göbekli Tepe might have been a paradise for the artists...religion and art are inseparable.

After I left from the office, I walked around on the spreading rocky area. Soon, I noticed some large lime stones lying on the ground. They had several cracked straight lines of a few meters long. Looking at them closely, I found many semi-transparent black stones of a few centimeters long were scattered next to them. They were hard and sharp obsidians which were used to chisel or cut lime stones. I immediately knew that this area's special geological characteristics in addition to its terrain were why a spectacle of Göbekli Tepe was created here. When I picked up a few obsidians to look at them closely, I heard a voice telling me not to take them.

On our way back, we could not find Gina. There were dangerous rocky area in the distance. Bűlent was looking for her. I also joined the search. Soon after, I spotted her looking up the sky and raising both of her hands behind the shadow of large rocks. Strange things looked normal at this site.

Many archaeological materials found one after another at Göbekli Tepe were temporarily stored at the museum in Urfa. The museum was located in the quiet section of the city. There, many ancient artefacts were placed outside. Some recently-unearthed artefacts were displayed inside of the building. I was told later that the government was planning to move all the artefacts unearthed from Göbekli Tepe to a new Göbekli Tepededicated museum.

As I stepped up the stairs of the museum, stone artefacts came into my view. First, I could clearly identify a boar among them. What caught my eye was a tall statue holding a baby. Its face and hands were clearly carved at the bottom of the statue. Immediately above the baby was a body with carved hands and breasts. The top of the statue was a large body with arms and a faceless head. They are perhaps the baby's mother and, maybe, farther. If the faceless head is not the baby's farther but depicts other being, maybe a god, it is possible that it was intentionally left uncarved. In any event, the statue was firmly wrapped around by two snakes. Unearthed from the ruins of Göbekli Tepe were not only the stone structures but also a number of stone-carved artefacts, including the statue of two entwined snakes supporting a baby, its mother and farther or other being?

During the Ice Age, many groups of Man lived in the caves or under the rocky areas. Snakes lived in and around these closed places as well. Because of that, there are many snake stories in ancient myths. The snake in these myths is often depicted as a symbol of a carrier of the spirits of the dead to underground because the snake sheds its skin a number of times to have a new skin, so that it symbolized a life capable to be reborn. The mysterious statue of two entwined snakes reappeared later. One of them was a small staff (wand) held in the right hand of a Sumerian statue unearthed from the Sumerian ruins. Another was a magic wand held by Hermes, a messenger of the Greek gods in the Olympus mountains, as described in the Hermetica written in the 2nd~3rd century. Following is a quote from the book titled The Masks of God: Primitive Mythology by Josef Campbell, a foremost scholar about the ancient mythology:

Dr. Henri Frankfort once sent an inquiry to the British Museum of Natural History. "The symbol in which you are interested may well represent two snake pairing," Mr. H. W. Parker, Assistant Keeper of Zoology, replied. "As a general rule the male seizes the female by the back of the neck and the two bodies are more or less intertwined...Vipers are said to have the bodies completely intertwined." "This, then," comments Dr. Frankfort, "explains most satisfactorily why the caduceus should have become the symbol of our god, who is thus characterized as the personification of the generative force of nature."

By the time the wand of Hermes in the ancient Greek mythology became widely known as the wand of Hermes, wings had topped the snakewrapped wand, which later became the wand of Mercury in the ancient Rome. It symbolized the world of commerce and economy of exchange and concession (negotiation). In any event, the origin of Man's symbolic consciousness embodied in the two-snake-wrapped wand was likely the statue unearthed from the ruin of Göbekli Tepe.

The Book of Genesis (Old Testament) narrates that Man became human after he cognized the good and the evil. It happened when Adam and Eve ate the forbidden fruit after they were enticed by a snake entwined around the tree of knowledge in the Garden of Eden. Earlier, they were warned by God not to do so. They ate it, nonetheless. This was the "original sin" committed by Man (or the "Fall of Man"). Since then, they were expelled permanently from the Garden of Eden since this time.

Snakes described in many ancient myths often appear as a fire god or sometimes as a water god, depending on the particular area's geology and ecology in question. These myths have much to do with the fact that life begins and grows as a result of organic molecules interacting with energy and water. Fire breathing snakes or dragons often appear in the Chinese mythology. Snakes in the Aztec myth breathe fire. During the Ice Age, Man lived with fire in and around the cave where a variety of snakes also lived. It is not difficult to imagine that Man remembered the burning pains when bitten by vipers.

With the arrival of Holocene, life began to thrive in the temperate zone. It was particularly conspicuous around Göbekli Tepe, where Man's new consciousness for his/her own existence was bursting out. There, a confident Man inscribed on the stone a pair of T-shaped anthropomorphic statues surrounding by many animals. This new vision of Man coexisted with a snake-entwined statue supporting a baby and a square stone slab (which may be the precursor of the "false door" of the ancient Egypt). As Man's control of nature spread over a wider area, a serious conflict was going to appear in this coexisting relationship, one to control nature and the other to coexist with nature.

Mysterious burial and surrounding ruins

After the spectacle of Göbekli Tepe was constructed, the entire site was buried underground about a thousand years later. The reason for its burial is not clear. It might have been caused by the increased development of the area to grow foods to feed more people (pilgrims) may be the reason as Schmidt seemed to suggest. However, there are many other possibilities. For example, as a result of the land development, there might been melees between the roaming hunter-gatherer group and the sedentary land-cultivator group. Also, small pox and other viral epidemics might have spread there. Or, a sudden massive solar flare might have created a sudden climate disaster (floods and severe cold) like Robert Schoch said.

Whichever reason there was for the mysterious burial of Göbekli Tepe site, a similar pilgrimage site appeared in less than two thousand years near the tributary of the Euphrates River, not far from Göbekli Tepe. The site is called Nevali Çori, where a temple and more than 20 structures existed for nearly three thousand years. The ruin was under water now because the dam was constructed. However, archaeologists unearthed many relics before the ruins submerged under water. Like the ruin of Göbekli Tepe, there were T-shaped stone pillars, clay figurines and other relics. However, unlike the ruin of Göbekli Tepe, they also found a dwelling structure. It suggests that caretakers for the shrine lived at the site.

There is no doubt that Göbekli Tepe was a precedent of Nevali Çori and also Tell Abu Hureyra, one of the Natufians who cultivated wild cereals as described earlier. At Göbekli Tepe, there were several large stone tubs, each of which could contain 160 litters of liquid. In the tub, there was a residue of oxalate. Oxalate is a chemical byproduct produced during cereal fermentation. I learned about this from the article by Schmidt and others after I received information from Jens Notroff who was in charge of the excavation work at the Göbekli Tepe site at my request. On the other hand, at Nevali Çori, there was an engraved relief of laughing people dancing with a tortoise-like animal and also a vulture holding a human head. In light of these artefacts and the shrine with some dwelling structure, it is not difficult to understand that the visitors (pilgrims) to the shrine of Nevali Çori were consuming fermented drinks.

These discoveries suggest that the visitors (pilgrims) to Göbekli Tepe, like those visiting Nevali Çori, were also consuming fermented drinks during or after a ritual of some kind. The ritual might have been presided by a priest. The reason is that archaeologists excavating at Nevali Çori found a stone-carved human head which looked like the Vedic priest's head of the ancient Indian Veda (Brahman). The head was bald except on the back which was covered apparently with a snake-imaged long hair. Veda (knowledge in Sanskrit) later became the present Hindu religion. A similar head shape appeared in Sumer as well as in the ancient Egypt where many people wore the similar hair-style.

All of these discoveries in and around Göbekli Tepe described so far likely upend the conventional view about the history of civilization: Religion came before agriculture, not the other way around. When the Ice Age receded, a mysterious spectacle appeared at a corner of the crossroads between Africa and Eurasia. There, people performed or experienced a ritual to share a newly awaken vision of the world and about themselves. As the number of congregators there increased, they began to organize and expand agricultural activities for more foods and drinks beyond the surrounding area in northern Mesopotamia.

Chapter 4 Symbolic Cognition and Nature's Fetters

Around 11,500 years ago, the freezing grip of the Ice Age began to loosen ahead of other places in the earth's temperate zone and a mysterious spectacle appeared on a hill in southeastern Turkey near Syria. It did not look like anything which nature created. It did not look like anything which Man had created before, either. It turned out to be a ritual site where people congregated. Having many new structures and artefacts, it was also a paradise for the creative artists.

True art has a unique power. Following quotes are from The Book of Tea by Okakura Kazuo: "Mind speaks to mind. We listen to the unspoken, we gaze upon the unseen....The sympathetic communion of minds necessary to appreciate art must be based on mutual concession. He thought about a true artist in this way: "Freed from the fetters of matter, his spirit moves in the rhythm of things. It is thus that art becomes akin to religion and ennoble mankind." At this changing moment of consciousness, Man's mind transcends the material or natural world and lives in the spiritual world of consciousness...Oscar Wilde once said similarly, "nature imitates art."

During the Ice Age, Man's cognition of self in nature was expressed as cave arts and figurines. However, the picture of self on the hunting scene in the cave art, for example, was often absent or drawn simply or vaguely only as lines or circles in contrast to those of the elaborately drawn animals hunted. As for the figurine, most are those of life-bearing women with exaggerated breasts and hips. Thus, during the Ice Age, most of the cave arts and figurines were expressed as what was seen by the naked eye, not as the unseen or abstracted in a creative imagination.

As the nature's fetters of the Ice Age became loosened, a new perception or cognition about the world began to take shape in Man's mind. Some confidently expressed it by symbolized structures and artefacts. A ritual stage was created to inspire people to believe that their life and the world around them did not happen by accident. It happened for a reason. It is also likely, for this very reason, that in the mythology of most later societies, the birth of their baby and society begins with a miraculous event in nature. However, as Joseph Campbell wrote, among many myths told, the true myth not only evokes awe but also explains about cosmology and social order and, ultimately, guides Man to spiritual quest as well.

Göbekli Tepe lies on a hill top from where one can see the horizon in every direction. In there, Man's new confidence was symbolically expressed about the hidden force of nature by building stone walls, carving spirit-imbedded stone pillars, stone statues and stone door. From there, a spiritual and symbolic world which transcends the material world began to spread in Man's world. Sharing and believing its meaning and message, Man became a stage performer (Homo Ludens). It heralded the dawn of the world of civilization.

Snake, wings and gods

As the new climate of Holocene began to spread on earth, many groups of Man in Mesopotamia left their dark fire-lit caves or corners surrounded by rock walls and began to live in the open space. At the ruin of Nevali Çori which submerged under water now, archaeologists found not only a shrine and a dwelling corner but also a stone-carved vulture grasping a human head as described earlier. There, the soul of the dead was not returned underground by a snake but carried to the sky by wings. The symbolized wings to carry Man's soul to the sky gradually spread beyond Mesopotamia. Later, a wand with entwined two snakes had wings on top, which became to be known as the Hermes wand in the ancient Greek mythology. Angels who appeared later in many myths and religions always has wings. Dragon in the ancient Chinese mythology has wings. In Tibet, even today, the sky burial is practiced to leave the dead in the open field so that vultures can carry the dead person's soul to the sky. The soul carried to the sky eventually became the shining stars in the night sky.

By about 5~6 thousand years ago, wings soaring in the sky became a symbol of the divine. Soul became spirit. Mythology of winged gods spread in Mesopotamia, particularly Sumer in southern Mesopotamia (today's Iraq). The Sumerians invented letters (cuneiform) for the first time in Man's history. This invention enabled others to share and record the information and knowledge at future times. As a result, Sumer could expand trade, technology and knowledge, all of which were indispensable for economic growth. However, as Sumer often fought with the Akkadian

Empire, the kingdom gradually began to weaken. Sumer declined not only by the war but also by the increased soil salinity of agricultural land brought on by the expanded irrigation. Eventually, southern Mesopotamia came under the rule of Babylonia (Old Empire).

According to the Sumerian mythology inherited by Babylonia, the first temple built by Man existed in the city called Eridu at the fringe of the Persian Gulf. It was the place to worship Enki (Ea in Babylonia). Sumerians worshipped An (Anu in Babylonia) who was the father of the supreme god Enlil, the winged god Inanna, the sun god Utu and the moon goddess Nanna.

One of the myths describes a person who lost a chance of immortal life. His name was Adapa. According to many scholars, this story was the origin of the Adam and Eve story who ate the forbidden fruit, the Fall of Man story in the Book of Genesis. Following is a summary of this story of Adapa who was given life from God but could not avoid death:

Adapa, a son of Ea, was given life from his father. Ea was one of the three great gods of Babylonia. Adapa was managing the temple at Eridu and secured bread, water and fish. One day, when Adapa was fishing, a strong wind blew from south and a boat began to sink, throwing Adapa into the water. For revenge, Adapa plucked the wings of the wind. Anu, the sky god, noticed the anomaly on the earth and called Adapa to the court of gods. Ea, Adapa's father, advised Adapa to wear a mourning, reject the offered bread, drinks or new clothes and rub oil on the body to atone in order to receive sympathy from the gods of the court. "Anu will offer a bread and water of death, so you should not eat or drink. Do not wear clothes, either. If offered oil, rub it on your body. " Tammuz and Gishzida showed sympathy to Adapa and calmed Anu's anger. Adapa followed his father's advice. However, Adapa did not know that the bread offered from Anu was not the bread of death but the bread of immortality. So, he lost a chance for immortality by rejecting it.

Rulers of Sumer acquired all of their power by oracle. At the same time, however, they were also destined to be subjugated by the teaching of gods. Near the Euphrates River south of Bagdad, there is the ruin of Ziggurat which was a massive temple where the moon goddess Nanna was worshipped. Nanna ruled the sky and the earth. In the ruin, there are tombs of kings and queens dating back to four thousand years. Also buried in these tombs were priests, soldiers and court servants. They were buried alive and their bodies were orderly placed with many gold and silver ornaments and musical instruments such as harps. In the ancient society, not only the rulers but also those in the inner circle also followed the teaching of their mythological god.

The glow of the moon and stars is particularly clear in the night sky of the arid Middle East. Nanna worship spread north beyond Babylonia to the northern Mesopotamia along the shore of the Euphrates River. In and around Haran, Nanna was called Sin. The name "Fertile Crescent" may also be associated with Nanna the moon goddess. Babylonia's precise astronomical knowledge such as the cyclical change in the position of the moon or the stars improved Man's understanding or cognition of the times, including the past, the present and the future. Later, it influenced the ancient civilization of Greece and Rome.

About five thousand years ago, the ancient Egyptian Kingdom emerged in northeastern Africa near the shore of the Nile River. The soaring pyramid of Giza and its protector Sphinx (half-lion half-human) was built during the reign of the 4th Kingdom. Today, the pyramid of Giza still stands tall about a few kilometers from the Nile River against the "red earth" (desert). It symbolizes the immortal life because it resurrects from the dried earth when the flood comes back.

Pyramids capsule pharaohs' tombs inside. The ancient Egyptian Kingdom was always captivated by the spiritual world. Its square-coneshaped structure was a Man-made large hill or mountain built with a countless number of huge stones. Over time, the Egyptian Kingdom gradually splintered. Most of the splintered societies were eventually controlled by many kingdoms or empires such as Nubia, Assyria, ancient Persia, ancient Greece or the Roman Empire. Nonetheless, the Egyptian Kingdom continued for nearly three thousand years even after the Old Kingdom declined. It revived first as the Middle Kingdom and then as the New Kingdom. Although many of the pyramids have crumbled, there are more than a hundred ruined pyramids still remaining today in some way.

Ancient Egypt consisted of many tribal communities where they worshipped multiple deities or gods (polytheism against monotheism) of various animals and natural phenomena. However, over time, the Winged-Sun god became the most important god. It symbolized Man's spiritual journey of life and death. Together with the Snake (Cobra) Insignia Crown, it also symbolized the authority of the pharaoh and his court as well as the sacred realm of the divine. Although the 18th Egyptian Dynasty briefly established a monotheistic religious system called Aten, an aspect of the sun god Ra, monotheism was an exception in ancient Egypt.

From the late Old Kingdom period on, pharaohs themselves became halfgod-half human. After their death, the ritual and oblation followed, which became truly grand during the time of the New Kingdom. They believed that as the withered plants regenerate with their own seeds, Man's souls would continue to live on. The burial room where the pharaoh's coffin was filled with many oblations such as the "Pyramid Verse" written in hieroglyph, a boat, arrows, wine, cereals and fruits. In the verse, there was a description of pharaoh's spirit being carried by wings to the divine world. Later, it became customary for some, other than pharaohs, to place papyrus scrolls of the "Book of the Dead" in their coffins. The scroll described the journey of the deceased to the world of afterlife. After physical death, he/she only enters to another world so that offerings must be made.

In ancient Egypt, seasonal floods took place over the shore of the Nile River every year. The Egyptians knew that the flooding always followed the movement of the Wolf star Sirius (Lord Goddess Isis' star), the brightest among all stars. Mysterious phenomena such as solar and lunar eclipses, aurora and meteoritic flashes and crashes intensified Man's sense of awe, which gave birth to many myths continued to spread.

As a new spiritual cognition and cosmological knowledge spread, more religious sites and rituals appeared in many places beyond Mesopotamia and ancient Egypt. Because politics and religion were blended as one, the power of rulers who worshipped gods was also enhanced. To secure the same vision with discipline was indispensable for maintaining social order. It was this symbolic cognition of spirits, wings, another world and gods that united or supported the ancient societies of Mesopotamia and Egypt. However, the revered divine reign combined with the deathdefying vision of the world also encouraged each society to have endless confrontations and tireless wars. However, as more destructions and deaths spread beyond Mesopotamia and Egypt, Man gradually began to contemplate about the meaning of life.

Good, evil and one god

Many of the contents and words described in the Scripture Avesta of ancient Persia were similar to those of the Veda (Sanskrit) of ancient India. Many believed that these similarities had originated from the Aryan invasion of the Aryan people from the Caspian Sea shore region into the Iranian plateau and the northern India's Indus River basin about four thousand years ago. After this invasion, the Aryan, Indian and Persian languages and mythologies were transformed in some way and spread beyond these areas. Many also believe that since this historical development transformed a number of local European languages, which are known today as the "Indo-European languages" spoken in nearly a half of the world's population.

However, archaeologists recently found a number of ruins of ancient settlements (Arkaim, Sintashta, etc.) in the Ural-Volga region of Russia as well. They indicated that the same mythology and living mode had existed in Central Asia well before the Aryan invaded to the Iranian plateau and the northern India's Indus River about 4 thousand years ago. In any event, according to Joseph Campbell, the genealogy of AhuraMazda in the Avesta and Asura in the Veda was the same as Zurvan Akarana who was a god with a snake, wings and a thunder-stone, and Mitra-Varuna who was a dual god uniting light (Mitra) and darkness (Varuna).

About three thousand years ago, the prophet Zoroaster was preaching Zoroastrianism whose god was a monotheistic (one god) called AhuraMazda. According to Avesta, Zoroaster preached that the chaos in the world was created by Man's continuing wrongdoing, deceit and death and that the lost truth and order did not happen autonomously. He prophesized that Man's good deed could restore truth and order to end the chaos and that worshipping Ahura-Mazda was the only way to unite the dual presence of good and evil in Man's world.

Zoroastrianism was gradually modified as it spread from the Iranian plateau through Mesopotamia to ancient Greece. Although details of the changing relationship between Ahura-Mazda and Mitra-Varuna still remain controversial, the clergy group called "Magi" played a significant role in the history of the East-West cultural exchange, or more broadly, the history of civilization. Magi was called the "Chaldean Magi" in the context of Babylonia and Hebrews and later also called the "Wise Men from the East" as they celebrated the birth of Christ. While it is likely that they worshipped Mitra (Mithra), god of light, in the Chaldean tribecontrolled Babylonia (New Kingdom), they undoubtedly possessed expert knowledge of cosmology and alchemy.

In Latin, the word "Magi" means magician. According to a Greek historian Herodotus who extensively travelled the Fertile Crescent more than 2,500 years ago, Magi was the name of one of the Medes tribes who lived in the west of Mount Ararat in the Iranian plateau and they had a deep knowledge about god and religious rituals. Also, according to Xenophon, another ancient Greek historian who travelled from Mesopotamia to the Mount Ararat region, the word Magi was used for the educator to teach the Medes's princes.

Most of the Medes tribes were unified by 2,600 years ago and founded the Medea kingdom in northern Mesopotamia. However, the Media Kingdom was short-lived as the chaos of war spread in the Fertile Crescent and beyond during this period. The widening wars weakened not only Media but also Assyria and Babylonia as well as ancient Egypt.
Eventually, Achaemenid Dynasty under Cyrus II (Cyrus The Great) advanced to the region in chaos from the Iranian plateau in the east and began to reign over the entire Near East and Middle East.

Magi continued their influence in the court of Cyrus II, where not only Ahura-Mazda but also Mithra and other gods were worshipped because Cyrus II's mother was from a Medes tribal family. He was clement and very generous towards the other peoples and their religions. Immediately after Babylonia came under his rule, he liberated the Jewish people from the forced migration from Jerusalem to Babylonia to work there ("Babylonian captivity") which lasted more than a half century after they lost their war with Babylonia...They experienced a similar captivity about two hundred years earlier after they lost their war with Sargon II of the Assyrian empire ("Assyrian captivity").

Cyrus II not only freed the Jewish people but also assisted them to rebuild their temple (house of God). According to the Hebrew Scriptures (Book of Ezra), Cyrus II issued the imperial decree: "The Temple is to be ninety feet high and ninety feet wide. The walls are to be built with one layer of wood on top of each three layers of stone. All expenses are to be paid by the royal treasury. Also, the gold and silver utensils which King Nebuchadnezzar brought to Babylon from the Temple in Jerusalem are to be returned to their proper place in the Jerusalem Temple."

It is likely that Cyrus II tried to restore the chaos in the war-torn Mesopotamia by good deed as taught by Zoroastrianism. It is almost certain that he did so because there was a fire alter in his tomb in Bazaar Qatar in Persia. In the ceremony of Zoroastrianism, the fire alter was indispensable. The same is true for practicing Judaism at the house of

65

prayer. Also, as time passed, it became increasingly difficult to distinguish Judaism's monotheistic god Yahweh from Zoroastrianism's Ahura-Mazda. For example, the following is redacted from The Dead Sea Scrolls (translated by Millar Burrows) which is the oldest Hebrew document:

God created Man to have him rule the world and gave two souls to Man so that both could walk together until God comes down on earth. Truth exists where there is light while deceit is born in darkness...One soul is always loved by God, eternally blessing him but God dislikes the other soul, even being near him, and abhors his deed eternally. Every truthful descendant would be ruled by the prince of light and walks on the street of light. Every deceitful descendant would be ruled by the messenger of darkness... God, until the declared arrival of the new world, knows every deed of Man. And God shall inherit the difference between good and evil for every descendant.

Cyrus II's administrative policy towards subjected peoples was based on clemency, which was inherited from Assyria. Later, this policy was also implemented by the ancient Greek city state Athens. In 2003, Shirin Ebadi, an Iranian Nobel laureate, said the following: "I am an Iranian. A descendant of Cyrus The Great. The very emperor who proclaimed at the pinnacle of power 2500 years ago that he would not reign over the people if they did not wished it." And......promised not to force any person to change his religion and faith and guaranteed freedom for all."

After Cyrus II passed away, however, there was a constant strife between Magi (Medes) and the Achaemenid Dynasty. Simultaneously, disputes with the ancient Greece in the west and other surrounding societies continued to mount. When Darius I came to power, the Achaemenid Dynasty-ruled area was at its peak. Soon after, during the reign of Darius III, the over-extended Dynasty lost a war with the ancient Greek force led by Alexander The Great of Macedonia and collapsed nearly two centuries after its birth.

The history of civilization as we know owes immeasurably to Zoroastrianism. It teaches that the chaos of Man's world comes from Man's wrongdoing, deceit and death and that Ahura-Mazda knows the life-long deed of every individual. Thus, Zoroastrianism teaches eschatology which is concerned with the final destiny of the soul. AhuraMazda is his/her ultimate judge (last judgement). This spiritual guidance for Man with a new vision of the world spread in the ancient world: Man must act to change the world with good deed. It influenced the teachings of Judaism, Christianity, Buddhism (Mahayana) and the Greek philosophy as well.

Man, anthropomorphic gods and Creator

In late 20th century, a ruin as old as 11,500 years ago was discovered at Göbekli Tepe located in southeast of Turkey. There, archaeologists discovered remarkable stone-carved artefacts underground, including a pair of T-shaped figures looking down at many animals, a two entwined snakes supporting a baby, a large stone slab (false door) and other stone artefacts. The paired T-shaped figures were anthropomorphized, which is a symbolic being to reign over nature. This pair reflects a dual existence. However, considering the baby-supporting two-entwined snakes unearthed at the same site, it is not a symbol for good versus evil. Rather, it is a symbol of man versus woman.

More than eight thousand years later, Man's cognition of the dualistic world became good versus evil as symbolized in Zoroastrianism. However, historical records about the prophet Zoroaster was almost none-existent, because they were destroyed by the army of Alexander The Great, Islamists, Turkish people as well as the Mongolian invasion.

According to Zoroastrianism, Mithra is an anthropomorphic god to be equally worshipped as Ahura-Mazda. Although the name Mithra did not appear in the oldest hymns called the Gathas. It appeared later in the scriptures of Avesta. Mithra who also appeared in the Vedic Hinduism (edited Veda) is an anthropomorphic god. There are documented historical records about Mithra, who was worshipped not only as the god of light but also as the god of contract. In ancient Greece, Mithra became the sun god called Helios, who was also an anthropomorphic god before Apollo took his place. Later, as the Roman Empire's reign spread, Mithra was worshipped in areas of Europe, including Scotland.

In the ancient Rome, Mithra (Mithras) God was born out of the underground rock surrounded with a sacred stream and trees. Freed from the fetters of nature, Mithras was worshipped as the god of light or the god of sun, a symbol of life's birth and growth. Mithras was prayed in secret shrine inside the cave or underground. These secret temples still exist today in Rome and other European places. In the ruin of the most elaborate temple among them, the bull-killing Mithras God was painted on the wall surrounded with a dog, snake, raven and scorpion. The painted positions of these animals correspond with the astronomical constellation of Taurus, Canis, Serpent, Raven and Scorpio as seen in the night sky.

Inside the secret temple, warriors of the Roman Empire pledged to Mithras God who was born by freeing from the nature's fetters of darkness. In this sense, Mithras was also the War God. Warriors who contracted with Mithras were allowed to destroy nature, men and women. With victory, they were led to believe that as they would reign over the world, they would help to bring social order.

According to some theologians, Mithra later became Archangel Metatron in Judaism because Metatron with countless eyes is an angel or agent of a god possessing the same divinity as the sun god to watch and confirm a man's contract with god. A few others think that Metatron in Judaism was also the origin of Christ, or conversely, the origin of Devil Satan. However, Christ who was born as Maria's child is different from Mithras who was born out of the rock.

Christ was executed in place of the Fallen Man and then resurrected as an anthropomorphic god. According to the Christian Trinity doctrine, God is the embodiment of Creator (Father), Christ:

And now we will make human beings; they will have power over the fish, the birds and all animals, domestic and wild, large and small...Be fruitful and multiply and fill the earth. The fear of you and the dread of you shall be upon every beast of the earth and upon every bird of the heaven, upon everything that creeps on the ground and all the fish of the sea, into your hand they are delivered. Every moving thing that lives shall be food for you. And as I gave you the green plants, I give you everything." (Son) and the Holy Spirit. Nonetheless, Christianity, like Mithras' myth, does not talk much about the nature destroyed by Man. There is no difference in this respect between Catholicism to teach Man's original sin and Protestantism to teach love. According to the Old Testament (Genesis and Psalms), Creator said the following about the relationship between the nature and Man.

As this quote shows, the Old Testament clearly depicted the relationship between Man and every living thing on earth. Later, the New Testament further clarified the relationship between Man and God as follows: Man created in the image of God is not in the figure but in the power to transcend self by reason, self-consciousness and creative freedom and in the will to realize them. Also, Man is different from animals because Man is capable to possess moral, mind and intellect. However, Man (Adam and Eve) committed the original sin by breaking the contract with God. Since then, Man always lived with a dualistic consciousness of good versus evil. Nature makes Man's judgment to err and his/her will to weaken, which leads Man to wrongdoings. Thus, according to the teaching of Christianity, Man is incapable to solve the dual problem of this world by oneself so that the unbroken faith in (contract with) God is the only salvation for Man.

After the Roman Empire declined, the vision of human existence based on Man's original sin and salvation spread widely in Europe until the 14~15 century. However, this inward-looking vision of the world also worked to curtail Man's desire to acquire and consume more in the Medieval Europe as a result. In the Medieval Europe, almighty Popes (Catholic Church) subjugated many European political rulers by excommunicating them and the Crusaders invaded many foreign societies to make them Christian. However, the leaders (priests, abbots, etc.) of the Catholic Church gradually began to put their own interests first. As a result, by the 16th century, the religious reformation movement spread in Europe. The widening movement gave birth to Protestantism which encouraged the believers of Christ to practice their faith without baptism or church attendance. Also, during the same period, Renaissance began to spread in Europe. This cultural movement resurrected the long-forgotten classic literatures and arts of the ancient Greece. Its propagation also owed to the invention of the printing machine. By the 17th century, many European people began to be freed from the Medieval societies' oppressive burden of the original sin and the aggressive political intervention imposed by the churches.

Nature exists for Man and the end of the world

About two and a half thousand years ago, Pythagoras who was called the father of philosophy came from Greece to ancient Egypt. At that time, Egyptian's mathematical knowledge had been extensively developed as it was necessary for the construction of pyramids. So, it is likely that the famous Pythagoras Theorem was born during this time. Pythagoras was also known to have coined the word universe or cosmos (σύμπαν) in Greek, which means order. Furthermore, he advocated that the origin of nature was Tetractys, which is a triangle consisting of 10 points. For Pythagoras, God became a mathematical symbol.

While Pythagoras was living in Egypt, the Persian (Achaemenid Dynasty's) force invaded Egypt. He was sent to Babylonia where he learned about Zoroastrianism from Magi. This is a historical fact which was documented by many ancient Greek intellectuals. Later, he taught the truth about the universe and the nature to many students in southern Italy and the Aegean Sea and Mesopotamia. They were known as the Ionian School.

Some historians think that during this East-to-West knowledge exchange, there was a confusion about Zoroastrianism---Avesta scriptures were likely misunderstood. In any event, the Ionian School tried to explain every phenomenon in the world by the Physis (Φύσις in Greek) doctrine, which postulates that nature creates the world. However, the ancient Greek philosophy gradually changed from the Physis doctrine to the Nomos (νόμος) doctrine, which postulates that Man creates the world. This Man-centric vision of the world was deeply connected with Zoroastrianism's eschatology.

About a century after Pythagoras passed away, Plato thought that Man's society could not be explained by Physis. Instead, he presented a new doctrine called the soul-physical dualism called Platonic Dualism, which explains that Man's soul (non-matter) and his/her physical body (matter) are separate entities. Naturally, this philosophy of Plato significantly influenced the politics of ancient Greece.

Plato's philosophical prowess was also in his vividly described cosmology (study of the universe). The following is from Plato's Republic: "From the fringe of the universe, I saw a streak of light which looked like a column was illuminating the sky and the earth. Its color was like the rainbow's but was brighter and purer. Next day, I saw the tips of many chains within that light. They supported the sky and the earth because the light was a belt for the sky and the earth. It supported the circle of the universe like the galley's under-beam. From these tips of chains many indispensable spindles are spreading widely...."

Later, Aristotle who was a student of Plato advanced Plato's cosmology further to present the Ptolemaic doctrine (Geocentric theory). Like Plato, he thought that the earth inhabited by Man was the center of the universe and that stars and planets circulated around it. Also, he was very critical towards Pythagoras and his followers because, according to their thought, everything in the universe could be explained by mathematics or numbers. Most importantly, however, it was Aristotle's new symbolic consciousness which separates him from both Plato and Pythagoras.

According to Aristotle, the natural world is made up with four changing elements (matter) of earth, air, water, air and fire; also, in nature, field, empty vessel and time permanently exist; and everything in nature is constantly changing between latent state and real state. He called his philosophy concerning this change as physics. On the other hand, also according to Aristotle, the celestial sphere is always in steady state made up with aether, not with matter, as in the natural world...every moving entity in that sphere follows a different rule from the natural world and there is neither beginning nor end.

The form of any particular matter varies depending on whether it is real or latent. For example, the form of bronze (matter) may be either a statute or a mere metal in the natural world. Likewise, Man's life and death are in two different forms but the matter is the same. Also, different matters combined exist in a new form. Following Aristotle, what is called the real state of an entity is the state where (field) and when (time) the matter and the form are inseparably combined.

Any real state of an entity always changes because power to do so exists. Aristotle called this power as the "unmoved mover" which is invisible but exists in nature. He cognized God or energy in this way. This thought transcends "dualism" because the "change" which is the essence of nature does not assume the existence of opposing or conflicting entities. This philosophical thought by Aristotle was later called "Hylomorphism."

Aristotle approached to the puzzle of nature better than anyone before with his theory of Hylomorphism. Nonetheless, he thought that nature existed just for Man. Following is an excerpt from his book Politcs (B. Jowett translation):

Now if nature makes nothing uncomplete, and nothing in vain, the inference must be made that she has made all animals for the sake of man. And so, in one point of view, the art of war is a natural art of acquisition, for the art of acquisition includes hunting, an art which we ought to practice against wild beasts, and against men who, though intended by nature to be governed, will not submit; for war of such a kind is naturally just.

These words clearly show Aristotle's vision of the natural world where the unmoved mover controls. However, Man was already awakened with this symbolic consciousness about the invisible presence of the supernatural power (unmoved mover, god or energy) in nature at Göbekli Tepe more than 9 thousand years before Aristotle.

People in the medieval Europe lived in muse. Their politics and religion were inseparable as one under the Catholic Church, which followed Plato's soul-physical dualism. However, Thomas Aquinas who was a Catholic during the 13th century discovered Aristotle's vision of Man and nature and incorporated it in the Catholic theology. According to Aquinas, every thought of Man begins from cognizing everything that exists is true, or truth in the world is one. This theological vision spread the idea that Christ was not only God but also human at the same time.

Chapter 5 Growth and Cyclical Transformation

Economic growth (growth) increases the production and consumption of goods and services. Also, growth always requires the increase of energy. This fact does not change with time. The word "mover" in Aristotle's "unmoved mover" in the natural world is the concept of God or energy. In fact, Aristotle called the power to transform the matter from real state to latent state (vice versa) as "energeia" in his book Ethics.

The definition of energy is not uniform even today. However, it is commonly understood as the matter's ability to do work. Its form includes heat, light, electromagnetics, etc. Our understanding of energy advanced by Einstein's mathematical formula $E=MC^2$. This formula shows the equivalence of the matter's mass with energy and also their quantitative relationship. It also means that, in nature, they are constantly exchanged or transformed. So, the gain of energy means the loss of the matter's mass.

The symbolic expression in science differs from art or religion in that it can be transformed to material technology. However, once it is technologized, Man leaves the world of symbolic consciousness and is brought back to the material world of nature. In the world of using technology, Man becomes just like any other animals to be always fettered by nature. Consuming natural resources generates energy. They are like the two sides of the same coin.

Sun, fire and energy

Homo erectus is extinct now but lived on the planet earth before Man (Homo sapiens) appeared. They walked upright and likely used fire by about 400 thousand years ago but they disappeared by the time when Man appeared about 200~250 thousand years ago. Man used fire not only for lighting darkness and warming body but also for roasting hunted animals. Use of fire for eating the hunted animals was Man's most important habit for the evolutionary process. Once roasted, foods become easier to eat or ingest. More importantly, the roasted food also made it possible for Man to digest nutritional foods effectively and preserve them longer. As a consequence, the teeth and lower jaw became smaller and the brain became larger. Also, in this evolutionary process, Man developed a new and different skin with less bodily hair than Homo erectus or Neanderthal. This new skin made Man to perspire easily in controlling body heat, enabling them to chase and hunt animals for a long time. These are biological characteristics of Man, a new animal species with a large brain. In this sense, the use of fire for cooking foods was the most important habit or technology for Man to successfully compete with other animals for survival.

The sun emits light and heat like a giant fire ball. It makes them circulate every day, day and night and their intensity and position change orderly in each day as well. Moreover, this cycle is repeated in every year. In many ancient societies, the knowledge about these changing daily and yearly patterns deepened with the advent of agriculture. In the northern hemisphere, the power of the sun's light and heat weakens most near the end of December. After this period (winter solstice), it gains its strength most near the end of June (summer solstice). At the same time, cereal plants wither and die but when their seeds are planted, they revive and resurrect near the end of March. There is no doubt that this knowledge led the ancient people and society to worship the sun as the god who powers the life cycle of birth and death. This fact about the nature of the planet earth led Man to symbolize the birthday of life as December 25 and its resurrection day as March 25. It is clear that this symbolism or religious belief is not limited to Christianity.

In the ancient world, Man lighted and heated mostly by burning the renewable resources such as dried wood, leaves and grass. However, as time passed, Man began to burn crude petroleum for fire in some cases. For example, the ancient Egyptian ritual at the Dendara temple lighted crude petroleum. Also, the ancient Persian force used fired arrows coated with crude petroleum. Except for these exceptions, the use of petroleum and other fossilized fuel resources was limited. However, the situation began to change radically as the organized society grew larger, developed and applied new fire-using technologies to produce metal tools and other manufactured products and equipment.

Power: from muscles to technology

When the Ice Age was ending, Man still lived by hunting and gathering in small groups. Man's estimated total population then was between one or two millions. Chasing and killing large animals required energy generated by muscles. The amount of energy spent by using own muscles is about the same as the amount of energy generated by eating foods. After Holocene arrived and the food resources increased on earth, the amount of muscle energy by Man also increased. As more communities in the Fertile Crescent began to domesticate large animals. They not only consumed these animals as foods but also used their strong muscles for cultivating land and building structures. Also, when agriculture spread by about nine thousand years ago, a number of settlements made up with a few thousand people each began to emerge.

With increasing knowledge accumulated in larger communities, new technologies began to appear by about 5500 years ago. Among them, wheels for transport and production and the metallurgical invention for making hard cutting tools and weapon metal--initially copper, bronze and later iron. They all significantly changed Man's world. They made it easy to move heavy things, produce a large quantity of products and construct larger facilities. As a result, not only the production of foods but also their storage became possible, which reduced time for hunting and gathering.

As these large settlements appeared one after another, their demand for resources other than foods also increased. As a result, trading timber/wood and metal products, domesticated animals and other resources expanded. Through these exchanges, new knowledge and technologies propagated and localized in many areas of Eurasia. By about 4000 years ago, the agricultural technology of irrigation and flood control spread beyond the

Fertile Crescent and the Mediterranean coastal areas. Large city states managed by bureaucratic organizations emerged in many coastal areas of the Indus River (India), the Yangtze River (China), etc. Their population exceeded more than tens of thousands each. Many of these ancient city states had military organizations and weapons to protect their irrigation facilities, water channels, bridges and other political and economic systems. In particular, Sumer and other city states in Mesopotamia possessed the powerful weapon technology. The weapon technology continued to be refined and improved with many repeated war experiences over nearly two thousand years. Each time these weapons changed, it became necessary to reorganize the military structure and logistics in response. History showed that Man's social organization and technological innovation began to change from civilian purposes for controlling nature to military purposes for fighting with other societies.

As the population and destructive power of each society increased, the pressure to secure more resources and territories increased, which frequently brought about the enslavement and genocide of other people(s). Most of all, the military of the Akkad Empire was so fierce that they conquered about a dozen societies in Mesopotamia. About 4350 years ago, Sargon the Great of Akkad had the strongest organization equipped with advanced weapons and armors in the ancient world. His soldiers wore helmets and body armors made of copper, dragon bronze swords and axes. Also, they used horse-pulled chariots with wheeled carriers, which were also used by Alexander the Great about two thousand years later.

During the Ice Age Age, Man used the fire energy and their own muscles to generate power. For a long time, Man's world was stationary until Holocene arrived, as agriculture spread, Man's economic activities, population and knowledge began to grow significantly, particularly after new technologies (wheels, metallurgy, etc.) were invented. However, as economic historians such as Leslie White showed, the transmission or transfer of major technologies which worked as the engine of growth in ancient societies slowed down as they spread widely after a few thousand years. For example, the bronze-making technology was transferred to the Japanese archipelago around 2200~2300 years ago from China. Also, it took about four hundred years more for the iron-making technology to spread in the ancient Japanese society.

Leslie White estimated that, until about two thousand years ago, the growth rate of Man's energy consumption exceeded the rate of Man's population growth for a few thousand years. However, after the mid-17th century, the growth rate of Man's energy consumption remained almost the same as Man's population. It is estimated that the Man's population in the mid-17th century was about a half billion.

After the 18th century, Man's technology and energy situation dramatically began to change. With the advent of Industrial Revolution, Man's population in urban areas grew rapidly, beginning first in Great Britain. Most important of all, the powerful energy-creating technology using steam and internal combustion began to transform Man's hitherto mostly agriculture-dependent economy to the industry-dependent economy. However, these new technologies had to depend on coal and other fossilized carbon resources.

Unmoved Mover and two futures

As the Industrial Revolution progressed in Great Britain, two contrasting views concerning the future of Man's world began to emerge. One was by Adam Smith and the other by Thomas Malthus. Both of them were leading social philosophers during the late 18th~19th century. As they possessed enough knowledge of the Greek and Latin languages, they were familiar about the works by Plato and Aristotle.

Smith wrote in his book, An Inquiry into the nature and cause of The Wealth of Nations, that the wealth of nations would come from the improved efficiency by the division of labor and international trade. He theorized that if those with funds engaged in business to seek their own profits by competition, industries would be diversified by the "invisible hand" to absorb many more workers and the society will grow in the most efficient manner and the wealth of nation will also increase. Smith's "invisible hand" resembles Aristotle's "unmoved mover." God or "energeia" (energy) is invisible but it brings power to generate and regenerate life.

The Man-centric "Nomos" doctrine represented by Aristotle's vision began to spread beyond the Aegean Sea coast from about 2300 years ago.

Before that time, the nature-determining world vision represented by the "Physis" doctrine prevailed in the surrounding ancient societies. Nonetheless, even then, their population growth concentrated in cities where the division of labor was spreading as well. In the center of such city, there were religious facilities and the offices for bureaucrats to manage taxation, irrigation and flood controls, and also many merchants, craftsmen and artists lived there.

On the other hand, by the early 19th century Great Britain, demand for coal for the steam and internal combustion engines began to increase rapidly. As a result, Great Britain's cities began to face increasing pollution from burned coals. Also, increasing was the urban poverty among many people who came to the cities from the agrarian areas. Against this background, Malthus opposed Smith's theory and wrote in his book, An Essay on the Principle of Population, that Man's population would increase geometrically but the food production would increase arithmetically. Based on this reasoning, he advocated that in order to realize a sustainable society, the investment funds should be made in domestic agriculture, not in industry, because there would be a limit for the population growth. This view was later called the "Malthusian Trap."

It is called a trap because, according to Malthus, increasing food production requires developing increasingly inferior arable lands which will eventually reduce the production yield per person below the survival level. As a result, the society's population falls into the growth trap from where it will be unable to increase more.

Man's world seemed to follow Smith's vision during the two centuries from the 19th century through the late 20th century. The "invisible hand" fostered technological innovation and international trade while the efficiency of economic system continued to improve. As a result, the production of foods as well as their distribution and storage significantly improved. Improvement was not limited only in the industrial production. Transportation and distribution networks also increased the market exchange (transaction) systems for services and money. For the last two centuries, Man's population and economy continued to grow. However, behind these developments, there were two hidden growth factors. They are the credit banking system (money) and the discovery of abundant petroleum (energy resource).

Growth and money

Adam Smith was not the first person to show that economic behavior to exchange things in the market would increase wealth and growth. Aristotle wrote in his book Ethics about the exchange between doctor's service and the farmer's produce. He explained that money was the answer to a difficult question of how to equate the value of goods and services in exchange: "Money solves this question. It is a kind of the intermediate amount of request and measures the amounts of excess or shortage in every exchange, and how many shoes are equal in value to a house or foods." Moreover, he explained that "money lasts long, easy to bring, divisible and valuable in itself." Today's theory of economics also defines money's essential functions in the same way as follows: a medium of exchange, a unit to account and a store of value.

Before money appeared in Man's history, goods and services were exchanged by negotiating without a medium. This kind of transaction (barter trade) also exists today. However, when agriculture began to spread about nine thousand years ago, domesticated cows and sheep or cereals which had intrinsic values were used as media of exchange. About six thousand years later, cowrie (sea shell) which is light and long-lasting without decay was used as a medium of exchange in some coastal areas. Soon after, metals began to be used as a medium. In ancient Greece, a stamped metal coin was used as a medium of exchange.
More than a thousand years later, paper or credit money began to appear.

Paper money appeared in China in the early 9th century. Although it does not have an intrinsic value, paper money can be made valuable by establishing people's trust in it by authorities. Paper money is easy to carry and its supply is not materially fettered or constrained by nature like cows, sheep, cowrie or metal coin. Eventually, institutions called banks to issue paper money appeared.

Banks could create credit money on paper at the stroke of a pen. However, if paper money is issued too much, not only the value of money depreciates (inflation) but also the trust in paper money will also be lost, particularly in international trade. In order to avoid this risk or problem, states established central banks to manage their systems of money (currency) by the early 19th century, first in Great Britain, to guarantee the banknotes' convertibility to gold, which has an intrinsic value. This monetary system is called the gold standard system. The United States established the same system in 1900 and other nations followed suit. However, as the banknotes' circulation and conversion to gold increased during the 1930's Great Depression, the amount of gold reserves held by central banks rapidly dwindled. As a result, central banks could no longer guarantee the conversion of banknotes (credit money) to gold and the gold standard system collapsed. Since then, the credit money system continued to undergo various reforms.

Today, it continues to be difficult for banks and central banks to manage the inherent risk of credit money, particularly in the increasingly globalized financial market. At the end of 2007, the chaos of the money market in the United States triggered a world-wide recession. Its impact has not totally dissipated even today. Also, the amount of exchanges of different currencies is enormous today. The fluctuation of exchange rates of currencies affects the growth and wealth of nations. Although the invention of credit money has fostered the wealth and growth of nations for centuries, particularly since the Industrial Revolution, history repeatedly has shown that the inherent risk of credit money has triggered economic chaos. Because the credit money system is a symbolic technology unfettered by nature, it always requires people's belief or trust in it. Ultimately, once technology or any knowledge must be physically materialized, Man will always be brought back to the reality of the fetters or limitation of nature of the planet earth.

Energy, urbanization and nature

Today, in the 21st century, living in the city is increasingly dependent on energy. Unlike the past centuries, energy consumption needs increased not only for businesses engaged in industrial production and transportation of goods and people but also for individuals and their dwellings as well. A numerous kinds of new electric and electronic products as well as air conditioners require energy to power them.
Energy demand is no longer just for lighting and heating.

Resources to generate energy are fettered by nature because energy generating technologies always require natural resources whether they are coal, oil, water, wind, geothermal earth, silicon, lithium, uranium, etc. Today, a third of the fresh water and soil in and around the rivers and lakes of the world, including Caspian Sea, Ganges River and Dead Sea, is already depleted or contaminated by economic development. Although some of the resulting loss of flora and fauna may be restored, few think that the radioactive contamination of soil and water can be cleaned up within decades as the aftermath of accidents at Chernobyl and Fukushima shows.

Electric energy was used to generate power for the first time in the mid18th century. In the late 19th century, a large-scale dam to generate hydropower appeared in the United States. Later, thermal-energy power plants using coals appeared. In the early 20th century, many large petroleum (oil) fields were discovered in the Middle East. As a result, many oil-based technologies and products were invented.

In agriculture, in addition to large gasoline-powered cultivating and harvesting machines, new oil-based chemical fertilizers and pesticides began to be widely used. Because oil resources and electricity were abundantly available, the size of each urban area became larger as many energy-enabled transportation network, high rises, etc. made it possible, which also increased the population density within each city. Seen from the sky, Man's world full of many mega-cities is now a shining spectacle at night.

In the early 19th century, Man's total population was about one billion and only three cities had more than one million residents each. They were Beijing, Tokyo (Edo) and London. However, today, more than 440 cities have at least one million residents each and some of them have more than 20 million residents each. Man's energy consumption now concentrates in these cities. According to the United Nations, about 80 percent of the world economic (GDP) growth during the last 60 years came from the manufacturing and services industries within the cities. There has been a massive population migration from the rural area to the urban areas. Also, a large-scale land and resource development continues around the urban area. Today, more than a half of Man's population in the world of over seven billion are urban residents.

As of 2009, according to the World Bank, the annual per capita energy use in the United States is equivalent to the oil consumption amount of about seven tons. This amount is about twice, four times and 19 times of Japan,

China and Sudan respectively. As of 2008, according to the IEA (International Energy Agency), the source breakdown of energy generation in the world was 33 percent for oil, 26 percent for coal, 20 percent for natural gas, eight percent for nuclear, eight percent for water, etc. For the United States, as of 2010, 25 percent for oil, 22 percent for coal, 22 percent for natural gas and 8 percent for water, etc. It is clear that if many developing countries, particularly China and India with well over a billion population each increase urbanization with high energy consumption, the natural environment of the planet earth will violently change.

Since the mid-19th century, the average temperature on the earth's surface has been rising by about one degree (Celsius) so far. However, this increase is for the average of the temperatures recorded in all areas on earth. In fact, the temperature deviation has become more significant. The more varied the temperatures of different areas become, the more unstable their weathers become. The resulting climate change mixed with extreme rainfall or drought is global, also affecting the direction and strength of the westerlies (jet steams) and the ocean currents.

The global climate change was triggered by the increased emission of carbon dioxide (CO_2) and methane gas mainly from the increased burning of fossil fuels. Much of these gasses accumulate in the earth's troposphere and encircle the earth just like the plastic sheet cover of the greenhouse. Also, according to the US National Oceanic Atmospheric Administration (NOAA), the rising temperature in the ocean in turn has increased the amount of CO_2 emitted from sea plants. At the same time, the nature's photosynthesis to absorb CO2 has significantly declined due to shrinking forests and phytoplankton in the sea. Today, nature's lifeand-death recycling ability has undoubtedly weakened.

In recent years, violent rainfalls, massive floods, landslides, forest fires and earthquakes occur frequently in many areas. The deforested and fireravaged areas are especially hard hit with floods. However, no area could escape at least one of these natural disasters. Most large cities in the world are now facing water (fresh water) shortage. So, many droughtstricken urban areas are increasingly relying on the underground water (aquifer). However, many of their aquifers have already dried up. This problem is particularly severe in Beijing, New Delhi and Mexico City.

The IEA and many experts estimate that the average temperature of the earth's surface will rise by six degrees (Celsius) by the end of 21st century. This estimate assumes that the current technologies for production and consumption will not change dramatically. However, there is no doubt that many areas near coasts of the sea and large rivers will submerge under water before then. In fact, many of them are already losing some ground. According to a report by the Asian Development Bank (ADB), about 700 million people in Asia will be impacted by the floods and the rising sea level by the year 2025 if the recent economic growth in the region continues. If Man's obsession for continuing growth continues, the life-and-death cycle of nature will eventually weaken to the point of no return, where the civilization as we know it will no longer exist.

Mass production of animals and plants

According to the World Watch Institute (WWI), the annual consumption of carnivora for food by Man is about 56 billion individuals (chickens, pigs, cows, etc.) or 280 million tons. Recently, these animals are increasingly produced at densely-populated production factories and those reared in the open fields have been decreasing. WWI estimates that the recent shares of these factory-produced animals in the total population are two thirds for chickens, a half for eggs, slightly less than a half for pigs, etc. Also, according to the United Nations Food and Agriculture (FAO), the consumption of fish and other animals (salmon, shrimp, tilapia, oyster, eel, tuna, yellowtail, etc.) caught in the wild (sea, rivers and lakes) have been decreasing while those reared by aquaculture continued to increase to nearly 42 percent of the total. The production trend for the vegetables is similar. It has been changing rapidly. Aristotle wrote the following more than two thousand years ago as quoted before: "Now if nature makes nothing uncomplete, and nothing in vain, the inference must be made that she has made all animals for the sake of man."

The symbolic vision of Man-dominated nature was born around Göbekli Tepe as the Ice Age receded to be taken over Holocene. It strengthened and spread in the world, giving birth to agriculture followed by many new technologies to grow Man's world. Since the 20th century, Man's population continues to grow as massive amount of foods continues to be produced not only by factories and aqua farms but also by genetic engineering. However, the excrements (byproducts) from the massproduced animals (cattle, chicken, pig, etc.) emit massive amounts of methane gas. According to WWI, the global warming effect of methane gas is about 20 times more than the effect of CO2. No technology is free from the fetters of nature.

Man has overcome small pox virus which spread as the domestication of animals. However, as the consumption and production of animals for food increased in the increasingly congested urbanizing world, new epidemic risks from a variety of pathogens and viruses emerged. At present, some of those risks materialized include Nipah virus (amphixenosis virus), E-coli 0157, Norovirus, Avian-flu virus, swinefever virus, etc.

According to the US Commerce Department's report published in 2010, the amount of energy used for producing and distributing foods in the United States has also increased to about 16 percent of the total energy use. Its increase grew six times faster than the increase of the US total energy use during 1997 to 2002 and its increment was about 80 percent of the total increment of energy use. In most developing countries led by China and India, demand for animal meats and dairy products is rising much faster than the United States. In fact, as of 2007, their consumption of meats already increased already to about 60 percent of the total meat consumption of the world.

Fresh water, like energy, is indispensable for animals and plants living on the land to propagate and grow. Naturally, it is the same for Man.

However, the amount of fresh water on earth has dwindled rapidly. Since the late 20th century, the sea level is rising with melting icebergs and ice sheets while the inland area is losing fresh water and the area's drought and desertification spread. At present, oceans account for 97 percent of water of the planet earth; icebergs and ice sheets account for two percent; and rivers, lakes and aquifers account for one percent. Already, Man's use of fresh water has been increasing twice faster that Man's population in recent years. According to US Center of Disease Control (CDC), about 70 percent of the increment amount of fresh water use in Man's world comes from the production of foods. This amount exceeds the fresh water use for non-agricultural production. As long as Man's obsession with growth for the future continues, the use of energy continues to increase and, at the same time, the loss of fresh water will accelerate as well. No technology will free Man from the fetters of nature.

From nuclear to deep sea and the Arctic

The great urbanization since the 19th century has sharply increased the demand for electric power. By the late 20th century, nuclear power plants have been constructed in a number of countries to meet their rising demand for electricity. According to the IEA, 39 countries have nuclear power plants to generate electricity at present. Some countries are planning to construct more nuclear power plants. In particular, China has begun a six-fold increase. Although the nuclear energy generation does not emit CO_2, the environmental damage will be almost irreversible if any nuclear accident occurs. Nuclear accidents already did happen. Just to partially clean up their contamination also proved to be enormous (Chernobyl,

Fukushima, etc.). The contamination will crosses over the national boundaries and oceans as well.

In recent years, mining the oil and gas resources has increased in and around the coasts of Africa, South America, South China Sea and Caspian Sea. Moreover, in recent years, the possibility to develop the oi and gas reserves is also taking place in the Arctic Circle, which includes the northern area of Greenland. As of June 2012, 97 percent of the glacier in Greenland has already melted. So, the color of Greenland seen from the summer sky is now brown, not white as it used to be. As the glacier of Greenland has melted rapidly, energy resource exploration projects in around Greenland continue to increase. According to the US
Commerce Department, two energy companies from the United Kingdom and Norway already own the oil and gas resource mining rights in and around the coast of Greenland. It is likely that it is a matter of time before their production will begin on the land of Greenland.

Large animals and people could walk across the ice-covered land bridge from Eurasia (Siberia) to North America (Alaska) until 12 thousand years ago. Even after the Ice Age ended, most of the Arctic Circle continued to be covered with icebergs and ice sheets. Today, however, the Arctic ice has been melting rapidly. As of September 2011, the total area covered with ice sheets and icebergs in the Arctic Sea was about one third (2,430 km2), down to about one third of the 1979-1999 average. In the 21st century, this enormous geological change on earth has been accelerating. According to recent research reports, the Arctic Sea will likely lose all ice sheets and icebergs within a decade or two. For these reasons, five countries (Russia, United States, Canada, Norway and Denmark) have already begun negotiating about their rights concerning energy and other sea-bottom mineral resources, fishing and shipping routes. The open sea in the Arctic Sea will no longer make it necessary for traders to freight through Malacca Straight or Panama Cannel.

In 2008, the international agreement (Ilulissat Declaration) was reached concerning the Arctic Sea development rights. It essentially determined that these rights would negotiated the bilaterally. However, according to the International Law of the Sea, any international issue in the sea outside the Economic Exclusive Zone (EEZ) should be decided by all countries, not just by the countries concerned. In recent years, it has also become clear that the ice sheets and icebergs in the Antarctic Circle are also meting rapidly. Despite the 1959 Antarctic Treaty and the 1988 treaty to restrict the development of the Antarctic mineral resources, Man is now facing another enormous challenge as the climate of Holocene is also rapidly receding since it replaced the Ice Age from the planet earth more than 11,500 years ago.

The fossil energy resource is the decayed piles of dead plants, animals, planktons and other living things which have undergone chemical changes over countless years. In particular, oil (petroleum) and natural gas have been created in the oxygen-absent underground with geothermal heat and pressure after more than a million years of chemical processes. Man has consumed much of the fossil energy resources during the last century or two. It is ironic that Man has found the way to resurrect the decayed dead in the underground and convert them to CO_2, which has been accumulating up in the sky (heaven) and changing the climate and geology of the planet earth.

Today, Man continues to be obsessed with the growth and wealth of quantifiable things. As this obsession keeps spreading in the world, the world is increasingly dependent on energy and money. It is similar to a driver who constantly pushes the axle and is suddenly forced to break only when the accident happens. The concept of growth does not just mean about the economy. Growth occurs in culture, politics and the spiritual realm. If the world continues to lose the life-supporting clean air, water, soil and climate, not only the economic growth but also Man's life itself will become unsustainable. Today, Man's journey which began around Göbekli Tepe after the Ice Age was ending is nearing the end of the road because Holocene is about to disappear. The following is an excerpt of Frank Knight's book, The Economic Organization, written in 1933 shortly before the World War II began:

Living is an art: and art is more than a matter of a scientific technique, and the richness of life largely bound up in the "more." In its reaction to the medieval and mystical speculation, the modern Western world has gone too far to the other extreme. It loses much of the value of life through neglect of the imponderables and incommensurables, and gets into a false conception of the character of social and individual problems. Our thinking about life-values runs too much interns of material prerequisites and costs.... The importance of economic provision is chiefly that of a prerequisite to the enjoyment of the free goods of the world, the beauty of the natural scene, the intercourse of friends in "aimless" camaraderie, the appreciation and creation of art, discovery of truth and communion with one's own inner being and the Nature of Things.

Chapter 6 Whereabouts of Civilization

During the Ice Age, our ancestors lived just to survive like any large animals. Hunters and gatherers, they were constantly searching for foods. When there was enough food, however, some of them expressed their inner thought about the mystery of life by carving stones or molding clay to make small figurines, and others hallowed the invisible spirits of animals after taking their life for food. With the arrival of Holocene, life began propagating under the warming climate. This visible change affected Man's life and the inner thought about their own existence in nature heightened.

In and around Göbekli Tepe in northern Mesopotamia, Man's imagination was leapfrogging ahead of other places. There, the invisible supernatural being in nature was created in the image of Man. Considering that large symbolic structures and statues were also created around it, it was in all likelihood the first anthropomorphic god and the site was a pilgrimage site. As the number of travelling pilgrims to the site increased over time, securing foods could no longer be satisfied by hunting and gathering alone. So, people cultivated the surrounding area for foods, mostly cereals. This collective behavior to plan and execute for a common purpose gathered momentum with the promise of agriculture. Eventually, those engaged in agriculture became sedentary and their settlements grew larger over time to become cities. However, Man's world that followed was shaped by how the society organized in response to emerging industries and technologies, which always required specific natural resources, particularly metals and energy resources.

Today, in the early 21st century, large-scale violent phenomena are frequently taking place in the climate and geology of the planet earth. They are spreading over the world as Man's exploitation and consumption of natural resources continue to increase. As a result, Holocene has began receding after having set in on the planet earth more than 10 thousand years ago. Because of this epochal change in the planet earth, nature's regenerative power has weakened in both land and sea. As the fetters of nature are tightening in Man's world, the social and political chaos in Man's world is also intensifying. Today, the future of civilization has become increasingly cloudy and murky.

Living in symbolic consciousness

Symbols visually simplify Man's complex abstract inner thoughts. On the other hand, a simple image does not reveal, by itself, what it means or the intention of its creator. It comes alive if it were combined with other information such as circumstance, location, time or space. The English word "symbol" is a combined word made of "syn" and "bole" of the Greek language. In Greek, syn means together and bole means throw. In the history of civilization, meaningful symbols nurtured the birth of religion to Man's world and later to languages and science as well. They also provide an important source of energy or guidepost for Man to live and work together towards a common purpose. Unfortunately, however, they also work as a source of energy to destroy each other.

Civilization is built on many symbols and its essence is found from the experience of people who live in it. The concept of good, freedom or beauty is relative and diverse. As Ernst Cassirer wrote, symbol is comparable to light because light reveals through its numerous refractions, different aspects of reality to people who live in different space. Symbols created in science deepened Man's knowledge about nature. Technology which applies such knowledge has the power to change, control or manage nature. At the same time, the more powerful technology becomes, the more changes it will bring to the organization and order of the society. Nonetheless, no technology can free people from the fetters of nature of the planet earth. It cannot be a guidepost for Man's inner consciousness for spiritual quest, either.

Symbolic consciousness deepened in many areas of the world from about 2,900 years ago, lasting for more than five centuries. Karl Jaspers called this period as the "Axial Age." It is also called the "Great Transformation" period. During this transformative period in Man's history, Man's morality-consciousness was awakened as ferocious wars spread everywhere, taking countless lives and destroyed societies. During this time of Great Transformation, Buddha in India, Confucius/Lao-tse in China and Socrates in Greece all sought after the meaning of life to stop the suffering of people and the chaos of society by religion and philosophy.

Shangri-La and Hakenkreutz

Sufferings from the repeated wars and destructions gave rise to a new cognition in Man of themselves in the ancient world: Believing in God would free them from the suffering caused by the corrupted nature. As described earlier, the origin of this belief or doctrine was Zoroastrianism's teaching of eschatology: Man's evil and criminal thoughts and actions stem from the nature itself so that Man can be saved only by believing in God and practicing their faith.

During the early 20th century, thanks to Industrial Revolution, many countries in the West and Japan were preoccupied with possessing and developing powerful technologies which could enable them to outcompete others both economically and militarily. At the same time, however, this preoccupation for economic growth and military strength also brought on creeping apprehensions for the future of the world. As the vision for the world constantly pursuing "more and victory" began to be questioned again, Man's symbolic consciousness to dominate and control nature also became cloudy. It made some of Man to think and feel that the civilized world might be nearing to the end...if Man continued to have such vision and consciousness.

Among these apprehensions, one of the most prophetic was a book called Lost Horizon written by James Hilton. It was published in 1933 when Frank Knight also wrote The Economic Organization in the same year as quoted earlier. Six years later, the Second World War erupted, following the Great Depression which began in 1929. Lost Horizon was written as a story told by a doctor of neurology: An airplane carrying four passengers, including a consul, from the United Kingdom and the United States began to head to China in the stormy weather from India (or Afghanistan). However, the airplane was forced to land in the unknown mountainous area called Shangri-La where Lamas lived. Having lost the airplane, they had no choice but to stay there. One day, the consul met and listened to a mysterious Lama priest who said he used to be a Belgian. The following is an excerpt of his story:

He remembered sights he had seen with his own eyes, and with his mind he pictured others; he saw nations strengthening, not in wisdom, but in vulgar passions and the will to destroy; he saw their machine power multiplying until a single-weaponed man might have matched a whole army of the Grand Monarque. And he perceived that when they had filled the land and sea with ruins, they would take to the air....Can you say that his vision was true?

Shangri-La was hidden among the valleys of the Himalaya far from the world of "civilization," where the melting snow flew into the streams over the Tibetan plain. It was a peaceful and beautiful Utopian society with a monastery. Soon after the book of Lost Horizon was published, Roosevelt, a US president, called Camp David (the presidential retreat in the state of Maryland) as Shangri-La.

In the mid-1930's, amid the Great Depression following the collapse and chaos of the credit money system (banking industry), Germany was facing a run-away inflation and rapidly rising unemployment, which bred a fanatic political religion. Being whipped up by this fanaticism, the German people began to believe that they were racially superior so that they should conquer the world. This political religion was known as Nazism, whose message was visualized by a hooked cross called Hakenkreutz. The objective of the Nazi party led by Hitler was to follow the ancient Greek city state Sparta where a group of chosen people controlled the society and conquered other city states.

The tragedy of the World War II ended in 1945 after tens of millions of people lost their lives, including those destroyed by nuclear bombs. Nonetheless, after this catastrophic hot war, a new world-wide ideological confrontation known as the Cold War began and intensified for decades. It divided Man's world ideologically, triggering a number of small-scale wars as well. During this Cold War period, arms race sped up and many nuclear bombing tests were conducted in the Pacific Ocean, near the Arctic and the Central Asia, including those of the most powerful hydrogen bombs in the Bikini Atoll and Novaya Zemlya. Their massive explosions actually shook the planet earth. Their impact on the natural environment continued through today. At present, nine countries possess nuclear bombs.

In 1951, China invaded Tibet and developed a vast transportation network in the Tibetan Plateau. As a result, it encouraged the Han Chinese to emigrate to Tibet while many native Tibetans there were forced to move to live in other areas. In protest, a number of young Lamas in Tibet burned themselves to death. At present, the tragedy of losing traditional cultures and territories of minority peoples is also spreading to Uyghur in the Central Asia where China's nuclear bombing tests took place.

The source of water of a number of huge rivers such as Indus, Yangtze, Yellow River and Mekong is the Tibetan Plateau. In 2010, the Chinese government announced a development plan for the area of water source in the Tibetan Plateau, including the construction of more than five dams in the Yalu Zangbo River. The rapid industrial growth in China prompted this project because China was facing serious problems not only of electric power shortage but also of watershed deterioration as China's aquifer and underground water was rapidly dwindling and increasingly polluted. Meanwhile, however, the melting icebergs and ice sheets in the Himalaya mountains relentlessly sped up, and they have already precipitated massive land slides and floods in the populated lower regions in Pakistan, India, Nepal, southern China and southeastern Asian countries.

Bonding on the wane

In the early 20th century, Max Weber, a German sociologist, expounded that the society's political economy was deeply connected with religion. He thought that growth and prosperity of the Western societies since the 18th century was an "unintended consequence" of the people's economic behavior guided by Protestantism, which taught salvation, a deliverance of the soul from sin for the believer. Weber wrote that Protestantism encouraged thrift and abstinence in contrast to the resource exploitation and the desire to consume.

According to Weber, the doctrine of Protestantism guided Man as an "ethical" servant to care for the God-entrusted assets. This religious belief would lead each person to become a profit-creating machine. However, by the early 20th century, the ideology of laissez faire without ethical consideration gained momentum in the United States: Only the freedom for profit-seeking individuals would bring growth, wealth and happiness to the society. It spread a culture of conspicuous consumption of resources or "the more, the better" in the world as if "the invisible hand" worked without Man's moral consciousness. After having experienced the Great Depression and the World War II, the government-planned economic system or communism challenged the laissez-faire capitalism to bring the social order and stability in Man's world. However, this ideological war or the Cold War ended up with a win-or-lose competition to outperform the other to achieve more economic growth because both unknowingly shared the ancient Greek doctrine of "Nomos" which states that the material resources in nature exist for the sake of Man.

In recent years, Richard Dawkins, an English biologist, advocated that the religion played an effective but dangerous role as it accidentally surfaced in Man's history. He criticized Man's religious behavior as a misfiring (misdirecting) of some useful instinct of Man. He also stated that the free competitive society was a result of Man's biological evolution so that the government-planned economic system will fail, regardless of its intention, if it negates the free competition.

For sure, every plant and every animal, including Man, adopts to the changing environment. During the transition time from the Ice Age to Holocene, Man was awakened with the symbolic consciousness in and around Göbekli Tepe. It was a true cognitive revolution in Man's history because the stage created to visualize the new cognition not only sparked awe but also bonded people as they shared the same symbolic consciousness. It brought on social organization to Man's world and opened the door to the world of civilization.

Today, the climate of the planet earth is becoming violent again and the social chaos is spreading in the world. Terrorism is increasing everywhere. During this globally chaotic time, will the Great Transformation emerge again in Man's world? In 1942, during the World War II, Kenneth Boulding wrote the following: "It is our duty to seek emotional truth, as it is to seek intellectual truth, and indeed as we seek them we shall find that they are not two truths, but one."

Geography determines psychology again

As of today, Man's population in the world is about seven billion. It will certainly grow more as the world's economy continues to expand. However, despite the economic growth, fears to lose local culture and social order are rising in many countries amid the globalized win-or-lose economy. As a result, a serious political chaos is also spreading and the risk inherent in the financial system for credit money is rising again as well.

The arrival of Holocene's stable global climate enabled all living things in nature to propagate as the fertile areas expanded widely as the Ice Age's frozen soil thawed. Without this epochal change in nature of the planet earth, Man could not open the door to the world of civilization. However, since the 20th century, the global climate has taken a turn again to the opposite direction. In recent decades, it has also become volatile as Man's carbon-source energy consumption has continued to increase from the spreading industrialization. The rising temperature has made the global climate to become violent and destructive. As a result, the nature's regenerative power has been weakening. We can no longer simply dismiss a once-regarded extreme view that Man is now a cancer cell for the living planet earth.

Recently, more social scientists are incorporating new knowledge discovered in neuroscience in their discipline as in the case of economics called neuroeconomics. The conventional economic policy just to promote growth may create more problems than solutions in the increasingly chaotic nature and society. A saying that "geography determines psychology" takes on a new meaning today.

Stardust in the universe

During the 1960's, there was a theory in physics about the existence of a special subatomic particle or boson which gives weight and shape to every existing matter in the universe. For this reason, this subatomic particle was sometimes called the "God's particle." One of the leading proponents of this theory was Peter Higgs. So, this particle began to be called "Higgs boson." In the 21st century, its existence was actually confirmed by a test conducted by the European Organization of Nuclear Research (CERN) at its huge hadron collider facility in the mountain of Switzerland. More mysteries of the universe may be explained by CERN in the future.

In recent years, Man has been accelerating the exploration of the universe by launching many rockets. Some scientists are seriously thinking about constructing Man's new settlement or a permanent structure on a planet outside the earth. Is it a Man's new frontier? Meanwhile, tens of thousands of rockets' parts or debris are now floating within the satellite-orbit ionosphere over the earth. At the same time when the risk of their collision with the orbiting satellites is increasing, we also know that the regenerative power of nature of the planet earth beneath the Ionosphere is weakening at the same time.

In the past two centuries, scientists gave us their answers to many questions concerning the mysteries of the universe and life. Even though they recently confirmed the existence of Higgs boson to give weight and shape to every matter existing in the universe, the hypothetical existence of the antimatter remains unanswered. According to the the theory of "Big Ban," the universe was born 13.7 billion years ago, and the unobservable antimatter is supposed to have appeared in the equal amount as the matter and had the energy of its own.

Many people were disturbed by the overreaching intellectualism. As early as the Civil War time during the 19th century, Walt Whitman, a poet, felt sick when he listened to a scientist's proofs to decipher the mystery of the universe. He wrote the following words later:

When I heard the learn'd astronomer,
When the proofs, the figures, were ranged in columns before me, When I was shown the charts and diagrams, to add, divide, and measure them,
When I sitting heard the astronomer where he lectured with much applause In the lecture room,
How soon unaccountable I became tired and sick,
Till rising and gliding out I wander'd off by myself, In
the mystical moist night-air, and from time to time,
Looked up in perfect silence at the stars.

The Peruvian city of Cusco was once the capital of the Inca Empire. It is in the Andes mountain range about three and a half kilometers above the sea level. Cusco has a well-known large Inca Museum (Museo Inka). In addition, there are four more museums in the city, including the Museum of Pre-Colombian Art (Museo de Arte Precolombino). In this ancient art museum, a few words written by Paul Klee are displayed. They read as follows: "I wish I was newly born, and totally ignorant of Europe, innocent of facts and fashions, to be almost primitive." Klee was a Swiss-born German artist who was assaulted by the Nazis during the World War II. They labelled him as a corrupt and degenerate artist and confiscated his art work.

The Inca society grew during the 13th~16th century in the severe natural environment of the Andes mountain range which stretched and soared across the continent of South America. The Inca culture is known for its in-depth knowledge about the sun and the universe. The ruins of Machu Picchu vividly shows the people's symbolic consciousness about their life in the Andes mountains. To construct its precisely-designed structures required Inca's in-depth knowledge. The chosen site was impeccably designed to show how the sun affected their life in the Andes mountains.

In the Inca Museum, there is a large drawing of Milky Way stretching all over the wall. Its detailed visualization overwhelms the viewer. It shows how obsessed Inca's ancient experts were with the wonder of the universe. No doubt, their psychology was shaped by the star-filled spectacle of the night sky against the sharp mountain silhouettes of the
Andes. In recent years, however, the Andes mountains continue to lose their white color as the glaciers and ice sheets have been melting fast so that their scenery looks different today. Similarly, the glaciers and ice sheets in the Himalayan mountains have abeen accelerating. Soon the Tibetan plateau is likely to lose its white horizon.

In 1969, Man saw the whole figure of the planet earth from space for the first time in history. Photographed from the spacecraft Apollo 11, its image has rekindled the long-forgotten meaning of Man's existence in the universe. Apollo 11 was launched by the United States during the Cold War with the Soviet Union, However, the image of our planet transcends the win-or-lose obsession because a startling image awakened Man that the planet earth floating in the endless space is a blue marble and that Man's life goes around on it by being surrounded by the shining sun, the moon and the stars.

When we look up to the night sky in a wilderness far from the city, we sometimes find ourselves as part of the universe. Sometimes, we are overwhelmed by this wonderous sense of our existence in the universe: time and space often converge as one. According to Einstein, time and space are inseparable. Also, the Tuvans in Siberia speak as if the past lies ahead because it can be seen while the future lies behind because it cannot be seen. Although both sound strange, it is true that Man's consciousness can travel freely unfettered by nature through time and space.

Standing on this hill of Göbekli Tepe, a music lyric suddenly welled inside of me...my journey from Göbekli Tepe was ending but my silent daughter was still there:

And now the purple dusk of twilight time

Steals across the meadows of my heart

High up in the sky the little star climb

Always reminding me that we're apart

You wonder down the lane and far away

Leaving me a song that will not die

Love is now the stardust of yesterday

The music of the years gone by.............. (Mitchel Parish's music lyric)

Afterword

I was an international economist for many years. Today, most governments in the world are still trying to promote economic growth by quantifiable targets as if such policies are the answer to every problem in Man's society. For the past 5~6 years, I have increasingly felt that most prevailing theories of social science would likely fail because they have been preoccupied with visible confirmation by numbers and lost a humanistic perspective or Man's invisible energy or psychology which bonds people together.

Back from the ruins of Göbekli Tepe, I feel more certain that Man's civilization emerged around this remarkable site. Man's cognitive revolution took place there as the Ice Age receded and a warmer and stable climate began to spread. Man's symbolic consciousness born at Göbekli Tepe was literally a maternal body because it gave birth to the world of civilization, which gradually bifurcated between the East and the West.

At present, most research reports about this ruins are naturally concentrated in Turkey and Germany. In Japan, for example, Göbekli Tepe is still unknown even among archaeologists. In the United Kingdom and the United States, however, the interest in Göbekli Tepe is growing beyond the circle of archaeologists in the last few years. Also, according to a recent news report, a number of research groups will be heading to the site. It is interesting to know that about a half century ago, archaeologists of the University of Chicago researched the area and concluded that the visible part of the site was created during the Byzantine time. In the future, there will be more discoveries and their meanings may unfold, including what the mysterious door-like slab was meant to be. It resembles to the ancient Egypt's "false door." The pharaoh's soul enters into the after-life world from this false door.

After having finished drafting this book, I received a mail from the German Archaeological Institute. It contained Schmidt's 2010 article which described about the stone-carved statue of two entwined snakes supporting a baby. He wrote that it resembled to the native American's totem pole found in the Pacific Coast of the United States and also to a lion-man hybrid statue of Leben Mensch unearthed in Germany before because the top (head) area of the statue had carved humps to look like the ears of an animal. However, Schmidt did not interpret the meaning of this statue of two entwined snakes supporting a baby.

Printed in Great Britain
by Amazon